Hang On To Your Hope!

By Ronnie Christian

Presenting Jesus
- He Still Cares -

Pen In My Hand Publishing

Hang On To Your Hope!

Text Copyright © 2005 Ronnie Christian
www.christiancowboy.org
First Printing October 2006
Second Edition - Expanded Version 2007

Pen In My Hand Publishing
P.O. Box 187, Blanco, Texas 78606
www.christiancowboy.org
For more information contact:
Christian Cowboys and Friends
P.O. Box 187, Blanco, Texas 78606
(830) 386-4936

Manufactured in the United States of America

•E-book available at www.christiancowboy.org

ISBN 978-0-9770325-0-1
Library of Congress Control Number: 2005906314

Front Cover Photo: Ronnie Christian in the Bareback Riding Event.
Classic Pro Rodeo - Horse #105 High Noon - Jacksonville, Tx
P.R.C.A. Rodeo 2001
Front Cover Photo by: Pfifer Photography, James Pfifer, Nacodoches, Tx
Arwork/Illustration by: Dale Hirschman, Jeff Young, Tammy Zamorano
Layout and Design by: Tammy Zamorano, Kerrville, Tx

INTRODUCTION: My name is Ronnie Christian. I am a rodeo cowboy who loves Jesus and wants to bring others to know Him. I am a member of the Professional Rodeo Cowboys Association.

VISION: Reach rodeo cowboys and cowgirls with the Good News that Jesus loves them and Jesus Saves. Through this, their families, friends, and the many people they contact around the world, including ranchers and others in the horse and livestock industry will know God cares for them and Jesus is Lord.

EXPECTATION: See people saved, set free, healed spiritually, physically, emotionally, filled with the Holy Spirit, and living a life pleasing to God.

Hang On To Your Hope

Foreword

Hang on to your hope! Every person in every generation has had the opportunity to be discouraged and feel like the situation is hopeless and then give up hope - do not do that; hang on to your hope! God declares in *Jeremiah 29:11 "For I know the thoughts that I think toward you, says the Lord, thoughts of peace and not of evil, to give you a future and a hope."* (NKJ)

In the rodeo world we have seen God move mightily among cowboys, cowgirls, their families, friends and fans. God has allowed us to see people go from despair to hope, from doubt to faith, and defeat to victory in every area of life. We have seen people, horses and other animals healed; people set free from drugs, alcohol and bad attitudes; families restored; dreams renewed; love, joy and peace become real. We have seen thousands receive Jesus as Savior and Lord and get purpose for their lives. We have come to understand that when Jesus went to the cross He took care of every need we ever needed. This not only includes getting us out of hell to heaven and eternal life, but also meets every need we have - spiritually, physically, emotionally, mentally, financial, socially, plus direction for life.

We have seen people baptized in the Holy Spirit receiving the boldness to witness for Jesus Christ and the power to come against sin, sickness, disease, lack, fear, Satan, his demons and every assignment of the devil in their life with victory as the outcome.

We have come to know that Jesus today is the same Jesus we read about in the Bible. Hebrews 13:8 declares, *"Jesus Christ is the same yesterday and today, yes, and forever."* So He is still doing what He has done before. He is the same - He still saves, heals, restores and puts hope back in your life.

God is not a respecter of persons. He is not partial. What He has done for others is available to you. I have spoken to the spirit of fear to go in Jesus name and have seen crazy acting horses calm down (even bucking horses at the rodeos) as we speak "peace" to them. I have seen bull riders with badly torn up knees ride pain free after speaking to their bodies to line up with the Word of God. Also pain has left people's back and necks. At a Cowboy Church service one lady was healed of arthritis, scholeosis and spina bifoda all at once. She left pain free with joy and later became the Sunday School teacher for the children. Another lady, a bareback rider's mom, was healed instantly of multiple sclerosis (MS). Many broken hearts have been healed and now the people walk in joy. Many with confusion in their minds have been prayed for and we have seen them get peace and begin to think clearly again.

My purpose for writing this book is to give or help restore your hope in a God who cares about real people with real problems and who has real answers. He restores hope in your life, in your dreams, in your future and brings you into blessings and victory.

Remember hope is always for the future - with hope you have something to faith for - so Hang On To Your Hope! - and - the blessings will come.

Ronnie Christian
Rodeo Cowboy, Cowboy Preacher
Phil. 4:19

We praise God for the impact that Ronnie Christian and his ministry have had on the cowboy world. From the early days of evangelism on the now PRCA circuit, Ronnie's heart has uniquely embraced all legitimate ministries; he has been both a pillar and representative of unity.

With a heart for lost souls, his magazine, Christian Cowboys & Friends, stresses this fact; it was widely circulated and well received throughout the western world.

It is our privilege to endorse and recommend his latest publication, *"Hang On To Your Hope!"* It will not only exhort, encourage, and inspire you - it will fill your heart with the life changing Word of God!

Glenn and Ann Smith
International Western World Outreach Center
(Rodeo Cowboy Ministries)

Table Of Contents

Chapters 18-23 are new in this Expanded Version

Hang On To Your Hope

*Without Hope You Are Defeated -
There Is Nothing To Faith For*

*Be of good courage, and He shall strengthen your heart, all you
who hope in the Lord.
Psalm 31:24*

Godly Hope Is A Sure "HOPE"

**Hebrews 11:1 "Now faith is the assurance of things hoped for,
the evidence of things not seen."**

Don't ever lose your hope. If you do you will have nothing to faith for. Hope is always for the future. Faith is now. Your faith stretches out toward your hope until it sees it come into being.

Never lose hope. When or if you do, you are done for. You won't be in a position for victory. Hang on to your hope. If you've lost it or seem to be losing it, ask God to restore your hope, plus refresh and sharpen your vision and purpose.

Worldly hope is a wish, a maybe, wanting to see a thing come into being but not necessarily believing or expecting that it will. Godly hope is a sure hope. You know that what you are believing for will happen. You confidently expect it.

What is hope? And where is hope? Hope is confident expectation, eager anticipation. Where is your hope? Is it in money, talents, education, a job, investments? *I Timothy 6:17 "Instruct those who are rich in this present world not to be conceited or to fix their hope on the uncertainty of riches, but on God, who richly supplies us with all things to enjoy."*

Where is your hope? It should be *"Christ in you, the hope of glory" (Col. 2:27)* Without Jesus there is no hope of glory. *Romans 3:23, "For all have sinned and fall short of the glory of God."* Glory belongs to God. He wants us to have glory on us but sin keeps us from having it. Sin removes it. Jesus' death on the cross and his resurrection to life again restores the glory because this is where He took and removed our sin. But we have to receive Jesus for what He did and who He is. He is Lord.

We need to be like Abraham. He focused on the promise and not on the problem. God told Abraham that he would have a child. Abraham (then called Abram) was 75 when the promise was made and his wife, Sarah (then called Sarai), was about age 65. Abraham believed God and 25 years later his son, Isaac, was born. *Romans 4:18 says, "In hope against hope he believed..."* In godly hope against worldly hope, he believed. *Verse 20, "Yet, with respect to the promise of God, he did not waver in unbelief, but grew strong in faith, giving glory to God."* Don't waver and allow doubt or unbelief in - hang on to the promises of God in this world. Abraham received the child of promise, Isaac, when he was 100 years old and Sarah was 90.

Romans 5:5 "And hope does not disappoint, because the love of God has been poured out within our hearts through the Holy Spirit who was given to us." It may be suppressed, but it's still there. Love and hope are still yours. By faith, believe for them. If you have lost them, ask God for them back - He will give them back to you. Ask and it shall be given. Remember these three abide: faith, hope, love (1Cor. 13:13).

Our hope is in God. Our hope is in His Word for: salvation, deliverance, joy, peace, finances, healing, soundness, protection, and, best of all, a home in heaven (John 14:1-6).

Jesus walked in tremendous hope. He went to the cross by faith in hope. His hope was to be raised from the dead by the Holy Spirit - the first born among many brethren (this had never happened before). His resurrection was the first with eternal life included. The same Spirit that raised Jesus from the dead will also raise our mortal bodies and give us life if the Spirit of God dwells in us. When we receive Jesus, our body becomes a temple of the Holy Spirit. We too have the assurance and the hope that we will be raised up to eternal life.

We have been busy spreading the hope of the Gospel of Jesus Christ to a lost, dying and discouraged world at rodeos, bull ridings, cowboy churches and elsewhere. Keep your hope in Christ and share your hope with others.

HANG ON TO YOUR HOPE. It will give you victory on earth and eternity in heaven. Place your hope in Christ. If your hope for eternal life is not in Jesus and you want to settle your forever destiny, pray this and mean it with all your heart: "Dear God, I am a sinner. I need a Savior. Forgive my sins and wash me clean by the blood of Jesus. I place all my hope in You now. I receive Your dying for me on the cross and I receive You now as my Savior and Lord forever. In Jesus' name, Amen. I am now saved. Jesus is my Lord."

chapter 2 — A Place Called "There"

Calgary
Ellenburg
Rapid City
Pendleton
Cheyenne
Reno
Denver
San Francisco
Dodge City
Las Vegas
Albuquerque
Ft. Worth
Houston
Kissimmee
Cowtown

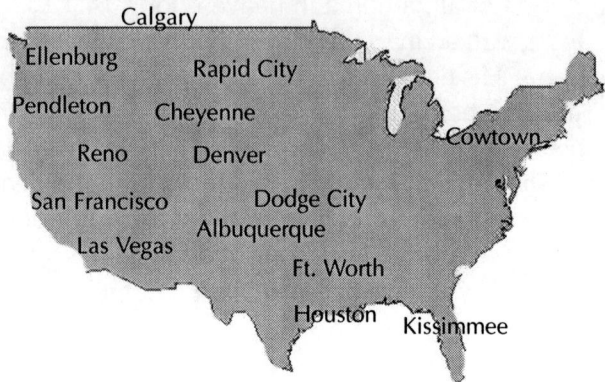

A Place Called "There"

Isaiah 30:21 "And thine ears shall hear a word behind thee, saying, 'This is the way, walk ye in it, when ye turn to the right hand and when ye turn to the left.'"

Have you ever felt like you are missing out on the abundant life and blessings of God? Have you ever stopped to consider that you may not be where God means for you to be? God has a plan and purpose for each of us. **There is a place called "there" where God wants each of us to be to experience God's best for our lives.** You may be somewhere, elsewhere, or feel like you're going nowhere, **but God has a place called "there" for you.** To find that place, you will have to *"seek first the kingdom of God and His righteousness." (Matthew 6:33).* Spend time reading the Word of God, the Bible, and spend time in prayer learning to hear and discern the voice and leading of the Holy Spirit (Romans 8:14, John 10:27).

King Ahab did more to provoke the Lord of Israel to anger than all the kings before him in wickedness and serving the false god, Baal (1 Kings 16:30-33). Because of this, the blessings of God stopped and a curse was prophesied by Elijah. There would be no rain for years and famine would follow (1 Kings 17:1). The king was furious and out to get Elijah when the prophecy came true and the famine came.

Then God told Elijah to hide by the brook Cherith. *"And it shall be that thou shall drink of the brook; and I have commanded the ravens to feed thee there."* (1 Kings 17:3-4). So Elijah went and did what God told him to do. The ravens brought him food every day, so he had plenty to eat and drink. Elijah was sustained right in the middle of a famine. But after a while the brook dried up.

When the brook dries up, folks it's time to move. So God told Elijah to get up and go to another place called "there". Verse 9 says, "arise, get thee to Zarephath which belongeth to Zidon and dwell there; behold, I have commanded a widow woman there to sustain thee."

When he got to the widow woman's house, he found that she had one son and only enough meal and oil left to cook one more time and she said they would eat it and then die from starvation. But then *(vs 13), "And Elijah said unto her, 'fear not; go and do as thou has said; but make one thereof a little cake first, and bring it to me, and after make for thee and for thy son. (vs. 14) For thus saith the Lord God of Israel, 'The barrel of meal shall not waste, neither shall the oil fail, until the day that the Lord sends rain upon thee.'"* The widow woman did it. Because of her obedience to give to the man of God first, both she, her son and Elijah ate for a many days (up to a year or more) as God multiplied back to her what she gave. Remember - *"give and it shall be given unto you."* Luke 6:38, and *"If you sow sparingly, you will reap sparingly, and he who sows bountifully shall reap bountifully..."* II Corinthians 9:6-11.

If we continue to follow the life of Elijah, we will see in 1 Kings 18 that God told Elijah to go again to another place and show himself to King Ahab, who wanted to kill him. Elijah called down the fire from heaven. Next he killed all 450 false prophets of Baal. The people then repented and called out to God again. Because of this they were open to receive the blessings of God again. It had not rained for three years and six months. Elijah prayed again and the rains came and the drought and famine ended.

In 1 Kings 19, God told Elijah to go to a cave and that is where Elijah learned to hear the "still small voice" of God for direction. Elijah continued to follow the voice of God until he went to that special place called "there", which is to be with God in heaven. God took Elijah up in a whirlwind, straight into heaven. *"Then it happened, as they continued on and talked, that suddenly a chariot of fire appeared with horses of fire, and separated the two of them; and Elijah went up by a whirlwind into heaven."* 2 Kings 2:11. Matthew 24:13, *"But the one who endures to the end, he shall be saved."*

Sometimes there are battles, temptations, and trials even in a place called "there," but God brings us through each one. But if you are not where you need to be - seek God's directions; He has a place called "there" for you - a place of blessings, victory, provision, peace, answers, and directions for daily living.

And don't miss that "Special place" called "there" - Heaven. Jesus said He was going to prepare a place for you in heaven with the Father. Jesus is the way there. *John 14:6, "Jesus said, "I am the way, and the truth and the life; no one comes to the Father but through Me."* Confess your sins and receive Jesus as Savior and Lord and go to be with Him and the Father "there."

ACCEPTING WHAT JESUS DID FOR YOU: Seal your destiny for eternity right now. Pray this: "Dear God, I am a sinner and I need a Savior. I turn away from my sins. Please forgive me of all my sins. I now accept Jesus as my Savior and Lord. Thank you, Jesus for dying on the cross for me and taking my sins away. Thank you for giving me eternal life and making a way for me to go there to be with you in Heaven forever. God is now my Father. Heaven is my home. Holy Spirit help me to live a life pleasing to God. In Jesus' name, Amen. *John 14:3 (Jesus said), "And if I go and prepare a place for you, I will come again, and receive you to Myself; that where I am, there you may be also."*

This chapter was inspired from a book by John Osteen entitled *"A Place Called There"* and also a sermon by Coy Huffman of Pro Rodeo Ministries with the same subject title, *"A Place Called There."*

Hearing From God!

(You Can Hear From God Yourself)

*John 10:27 My sheep hear My voice and I know them, and
they follow Me; (28) and I give eternal life to them,
and they shall never perish;
and no one shall snatch them out of My hand.
Signed Jesus*

Hearing From God.
It's time for YOU to hear from the Holy Ghost.

*1 John 2:27 "And as for you, the anointing which you received
from Him (God) abides in you, and you have no need for anyone to teach you; but as His anointing teaches you about all
things, and is true and is not a lie, and just as it has taught you,
you abide in Him."*

This does not mean you shouldn't listen and learn from good Bible teachers. Thank God for anointed preachers and teachers of His word. Thank God for the fivefold ministry mentioned in *Ephesians 4:11: "And He gave some as apostles, and some as prophets, and some as evangelists, and some as pastors and teachers (12) for the equipping of the saints for the work of service, to the building up of the body of Christ..."* God has given us men and women anointed by the Holy Spirit to teach us and help us. As we are taught **we should learn to hear from the Holy**

Spirit ourselves. Your preacher, parents and Christian friends cannot give you every answer you need to hear and know all the time. The Holy Spirit will speak to you personally and guide you into all truth and you will be able to recognize a lie and pitfalls and those who masquerade bad as good and wrong as right. Learn to hear the voice of God; ask Him for discernment when making decisions about direction for your life - whether a thing be right or wrong, good or bad for you.

Be willing to ask of God, and then be still long enough to listen, and then be willing to do what He says, and then be obedient enough to follow His direction.

1 Kings 3:5-14, Solomon as a young man became King over Israel. He knew he needed God's help in ruling the people. God asked Solomon in a dream, "Ask! What shall I give you?" It is commonly taught that Solomon asked for wisdom. But in actuality, Solomon asked for an understanding heart; the original Hebrew says **he asked for a "hearing heart"** to judge the people so that he could discern between good and evil. (The report in II Chron. 1:10 is Solomon did say, "Now give me wisdom and knowledge.") Anyway, God gave him wisdom above all others and an understanding or a **"hearing heart"** and because of his unselfish request, both riches and honor, more than any of the kings before or after him.

Oh, that God would give us a hearing heart so that we will hear and know His voice, to understand what the will of the Lord is, to keep us in righteousness and guide our every thought and decision, to draw us close to Him and grant us peace.

Understand that the Holy Ghost (or Holy Spirit if you prefer) will **lead you**, will **speak to you**, will **help you**, will **draw you to God** and will **keep you**.

Remember Solomon's hearing heart. You can have one too. *Proverbs 23:7 "For as he thinketh in his heart, so is he..."* God knows what is in your heart. The Holy Spirit will speak to your heart and give you good thoughts. Receive them. Receive Him!

Let's look at a few scriptures about the Holy Spirit.

8

Romans 8:14 "For all who are being led by the Spirit of God, these are sons of God." Vs 16 "The Spirit Himself bears witness with our spirit that we are children of God."

*John 14:26 "But the Comforter (the Helper), the Holy Spirit, whom the Father will send in My (Jesus') name, **He will teach you all things, and bring to rememberance** all that I said to you." Vs 27 "Peace I leave with you..."* (the Holy Spirit brings peace to you.) The Holy Spirit is our helper; our "Paracletos", which means one called alongside to help.

John 16:8 "And He, when He comes, will convict the world concerning sin, and righteousness and judgement." He will convict you of sin so you will confess it, get forgiven of it, and get out of it.

*John 16:13 "But when He, the Spirit of truth comes, He will guide you into all the truth; for He will not speak on His own initiative, but whatever He hears, **He will speak;** and He will disclose to you what is to come."*

In closing - What are some things we can do to listen to and be led by the Holy Spirit. There are a few very basic things to do. (1) Pray every day. (2) Read your Bible every day. (3) Spend some quiet time alone with God. (4) Fellowship with other believers often. (5) Praise and worship the Father. (6) Listen to good sound teaching from those anointed of God to minister. (7) Ask Him to speak to you. Luke 11:9-10. (8) In certain situations you may need to pray and fast. (9) Be filled with the Holy Spirit.

If you know Jesus as Lord and God as your Father you have the Holy Spirit. If you need to be filled to overflowing and **need the boldness to carry out His direction for you life,** ask your Father for this. Luke 11:13 It's another experience with the Holy Spirit. It is being baptized (totally immersed) in the Holy Spirit. Jesus is the Baptizer in the Holy Spirit. Mark 1:8. Acts 1:8, 4:31, 8:14-16, Acts 10:43-46, Romans 8:26.

Acts 4:31 "And when they had prayed, the place where they had gathered together was shaken, and they were all filled with the Holy Spirit, and began to speak the word of God with boldness."

9

Prayer should be a dialogue when you not only speak but listen - a conversation.

HEARING FROM THE HOLY GHOST: Do you know you are saved? Have you asked God to forgive you for your sins? Have you received Jesus as your Savior? Jesus is the only way to God. *John 14:6 "Jesus said to him, I am the way, and the truth, and the life; no one comes to the Father, but through Me."* He shed His blood and died on the cross and rose again for your sin. He made a way for you to go to Heaven and live forever. Is the Holy Ghost telling you to repent (change) and ask forgiveness of sins in your life. Listen to Him. Do it now. Pray a prayer like this -

Dear God, have mercy on me, the sinner. I confess my sins and ask you to forgive me and I turn away from sin. I turn to You and accept Jesus as my Savior and Lord. I ask You, Jesus, to baptize me in the Holy Spirit, fill me with Your love and the boldness to be what You want me to be. Dear Holy Spirit, talk to me and guide me all the days of my life. I thank You. In Jesus' name. Amen.

Benefits For You At The Cross

(When Jesus
Went To The
Cross He Took
Care Of Every
Need That We
Ever Needed)

Jesus said, "It is finished." John 19:30

The Finished Work Of The Cross
And The Blood Of Jesus!

I Corinthians 1:18 "for the preaching of the cross is to them that perish foolishness; but unto us which are saved it is the power of God."

The world does not understand why the cross of Calvary on which Jesus bore our sins and died is so important. Without the crucifixion of Jesus on the cross we would have no forgiveness of sins. We would not have a way to Heaven. God would still be our Creator, but not our Father. When we accept Jesus as Savior and Lord we can then cry out to God saying *"Abba! Father!"* (Romans 8:16, Galatians 4:6) Jesus said, *"If you had known Me, you would have known My Father also;..."* John 14:7

It may sound foolish to some. But who does it sound foolish to? Those who are perishing! But unto the believer in Christ and His finished work on the cross it is the power of God. That same power of the Holy Spirit that raised Jesus from the dead will also quicken our bodies and raise us from the dead and give us a home in heaven with new bodies that will never die. And if you are still alive when the Lord comes you will be caught up (or raptured) to meet the Lord in the air (after those who are dead in Christ have been raised first) 1 Thes. 4:17.

So you see, **it's pretty exciting for Christians when we think about the cross.** We understand that Jesus died in our place. The only one who was sinless became sin for us and died for us. *II Corinthians 5:21 "He made Him who knew no sin be sin on our behalf, that we might become the righteousness of God in Him."*

When we ask forgiveness and repent God looks down from Heaven and sees the Blood of Jesus covering us. **The Blood cleanses us.** Thank you Jesus for being obedient and going to the cross for us.

Philippians 2:8 "and being found in appearance as a man, He (Jesus) humbled himself by becoming obedient to the point of death, even death on the cross. (9) Therefore God highly exalted Him, and bestowed on Him the name which is above every name. (10) that at the name of Jesus every knee should bow, of those in heaven, and on earth, and under the earth (11) and that every tongue should confess that Jesus Christ is Lord to the glory of God the Father."

Not only does the work of the cross get us a way to Heaven, but there is much more. Read all of Isaiah 53 where it prophesies about the crucifixion 100's of years before it took place.

When Jesus died on the cross, He took care of every need that we ever needed. The most important is the salvation of our spirit and soul. However, he did much more than that. He took care of us spiritually, physically, emotionally, financially, socially, and every other way.

If you check out the word salvation, you will see that it means protection, healing, soundness, prosperity, and deliverance from every kind of evil. Everything Adam lost in the garden of Eden, Jesus won it back on the cross

If your enemy, the devil, is coming against you, resist him and he will flee and remember *Revelation 12:11 "And they overcame him (the devil) because of the blood of the Lamb (Jesus) and because of the word of their testimony, and they did not love their life even in death."* So we see we overcome the devil because of the shedding of the Blood of Jesus on the cross. We know of stories where people's lives have been spared because someone prayed and would plead the Blood of Jesus over them. We know of stories of would-be rape victims who would say "I plead the Blood of Jesus!" and their would be rapist ran off in fear. **There is power in the Blood.**

II Peter 2:24 "and He Himself bore our sins in His body on the cross, that we might die to sin and live to righteousness for by His stripes we are healed." While this refers to the healing of our souls most importantly, many, many people have claimed this Scripture and received physical healing (See Isaiah 53 again).

When my son, Caleb, was about 7 or 8 days old and he was in the intensive care unit at the hospital, he turned purple and the doctors did C.P.R. on him for 20 minutes. The doctor came out to see me to explain what had happened. I took her by the hands and prayed a prayer I had never prayed before. I said, "Father, when your Son, Jesus, went to the cross he took care of every need we ever needed and I thank you." Within an hour the doctors said he was actually better off than before the episode. At least his lungs finally opened. (They had shut down a few hours after his birth.) He grew up healthy and strong.

The finished work of the cross is so much more vast in the blessings we receive than we can cover in this article.

One more thing though, is that because Jesus died for us and went away He sent us the Holy Spirit, our Helper, our Comforter. He is the Spirit of truth. He will lead you, guide you, be with you and help you in every need. The Holy Spirit will give you power to live a life pleasing to God and to be an overcomer.

ACCEPTING WHAT JESUS DID FOR YOU: Let's pray, "Dear God, thank you for giving us your Son. Dear Jesus, thank you for shedding your Blood on the cross for me. Thank you for forgiving me of my sins. I accept what you did on the cross for me. I receive you as my Savior and confess You as Lord of my life. Thank you for giving me a home in Heaven. Thank you for taking care of every need I will ever have. In Jesus' name. Amen.

Forgiveness - A Must

(If You Don't Forgive Others -
God Won't Forgive You)

MATTHEW 6:14-15 "For if you forgive men for their transgressions, your heavenly Father will also forgive you. (15) But if you do not forgive men, then your Father will not forgive your transgressions."

The above verses come just after what is known to many as the Lord's Prayer or to some it is called the disciples prayer where it says in *Matthew 6:12 "And forgive us our debts (trespasses), as we forgive our debtors."*

God declares you must forgive in order to be forgiven. This is serious. There are thousands of people "bound up today in unforgiveness." This includes the believers in Christ Jesus. But unforgiveness is not an option. You must forgive others. Unforgiveness blocks your prayers and your blessings.

CHOOSE TO FORGIVE and your feelings will catch up later. You say you don't feel like forgiving someone, when they did you wrong. They don't deserve being forgiven. Well even if they did you wrong, nobody in this world is worth messing up your relationship with the Lord, no matter what they did. So choose to forgive by an act of your will and your feelings will have to catch up later.

You may not trust them but you must forgive them; Trust takes time. Forgiveness is a must, but trust is earned. Trust takes time. Forgiveness is immediate. Unforgiveness goes to bitterness, which goes to rebellion, which goes to hate. I've observed this pattern time and time again. Unforgiveness can wreck your life. Anger comes from hurt. You say, "No I am just mad." No, you are hurt. But if you don't forgive, you are living in unforgiveness. Unforgiveness is a sin and if you hold it long enough it turns into bitterness. The Bible declares that the root of bitterness springs up and causes trouble. (Heb 12:15). Bitterness is like cancer; it will eat up the one who has it. If you live with bitterness, it will turn to rebellion. Rebellion is "like the sin of witchcraft" (See I

But unforgiveness is not an option.
You must forgive others.
Unforgiveness blocks your prayers and your blessings.
CHOOSE TO FORGIVE
and your feelings will catch up later.

Sam. 15:23). It brings the same results as witchcraft - it is destructive. A person in rebellion rebels against their spouse, their parents, the government authorities, the leaders in the church, against those in authority, against what is right, against the Word of God and actually against God Himself. This will bring about curses not blessings in your life. This place of unforgiveness, bitterness and the rebellion cause enough trouble yet there is another place it will take you - and that is HATE. God is love and the farthest you can get from God is hate. Hate destroys lives but most of all it destroys the one who carries it. So you see, it is best to forgive and not go through all these stages. When you forgive, the process is reversed. All the hate, rebellion, bitterness and unforgiveness, and hurt leaves so you can once again be close to God, pleasing Him and opening up yourself for blessings. You will walk in love again.

So choose to forgive and be free from all the destructive things that go with unforgiveness.

When you don't forgive you are someone else's slave. How long do you want to be a slave to them? You think about them too much, you let it steal your joy, you stress out, they occupy your mind and your time. You are in bondage to them. You are their slave. It's time to be free. Unforgiveness is a sin. *John 8:32 "'and you shall know the truth and the truth shall set you free. (v34) Jesus answered them, 'Truly, truly, I say to you, everyone who commits sin is a slave of sin, (35) And the slave does not remain in the house forever; the Son does remain forever (36) If therefore the Son shall make you free, you shall be free indeed.'"* Jesus came to set you free - forgive and be free.

There is another step you can take. This may be tough but it will bring you peace and joy and blessings. Forgive, then, ask God to bless them. The Bible says to *"bless those who curse you, and pray for those who mistreat you." (Luke 6:28)* That is what Jesus does to us; He forgives us then blesses us. He even forgets the sin. *Jeremiah 31:34 "...For I will forgive their iniquity, and their sin I will remember no more."* We can even reach that point and forget about it or at least we can remember without the hurt and anger anymore.

Someone may have caused you much trouble. The situation caused you a lot of trouble, stress, time and concern. It is a care of yours. Give your cares to God, He can handle them, He can handle the situation, He can handle the people involved. Let God take the cares. *I Peter 5:7 "casting all your cares (anxiety) upon Him, because He cares for you."* He can handle all of your cares if you release them to Him. Make a trade - trade Jesus your cares for His load. Your cares are heavy, His load is light. Your care brings stress, His load brings rest. (Mat. 11:28-30)

Jesus talked in Mark 11:23-24 about casting your mountains into the sea, He goes on to say that we can have all things for which we pray and ask when we believe. Then He says in *vs 25 "And whenever you stand praying, forgive, if you have anything against anyone; so that your Father also who is in heaven may forgive you your transgressions. (26) But if you do not forgive, neither will your Father who is in heaven forgive your transgressions."*

Forgiveness is not an option - it is a must. When you forgive, you become free from the person and you walk out of bitterness, rebellion and even hate, back to joy, love and a good relationship with the Father.

If the Holy Spirit brings up a person or persons to you as you read this that you need to forgive, do so right now. Say, "Father I forgive them, you deal with them and also with me. Bless them Lord. You died for them too. Help them to be what you desire them to be." In Jesus Name I pray.

FORGIVENESS - What about you? Do you need forgiveness from God. *I John 1:9 "If we confess our sins, He is faithful and righteous to forgive us our sins and to cleanse us from all unrighteousness."* If you want God's forgiveness and you want to live eternally with God pray this. "Dear God, I am a sinner, I need a Savior. I ask You to forgive me of my sins now. I receive what Jesus did for me when He hung on the cross for my sins. I receive Jesus into my heart right now as Savior and Lord. Thank You for forgiving me and giving me life eternal. Holy Spirit help me to live a life pleasing to my Father in heaven. In Jesus name, I pray. Amen" (See Romans 3:10, 3:23, 5:8, 6:23, 10:9 &10, 13, John 3:16, Acts 2:38.)

HOW MANY TIMES MUST I FORGIVE?
Matthew 18:21-22
Then Peter came to Him and said, "Lord, how often shall my brother sin against me, and I forgive him? Up to seven times?" (22) Jesus said to him, "I do not say to you, up to seven times, but up to seventy times seven."

This passage talks about a slave who was forgiven by the King for a very large debt! However the slave went out but would not forgive his fellow slave a very small debt. When the King heard about his action, he scolded the slave and said *(vs 32), "I forgave you all that debt... (33) Should you not also have had mercy on your fellow slave, even as I have had mercy on you!"* He was moved with anger and handed him over to the torturers. *Verse 35 "So shall My heavenly Father also do to you, if each of you does not forgive his brother from your heart."*

70 X 7

6

Decisions...
Decisions...
Follow Peace

Road of Turmoil   Road of Peace

Road of Decision

Psalm 34:14
... Seek peace
and
pursue it.

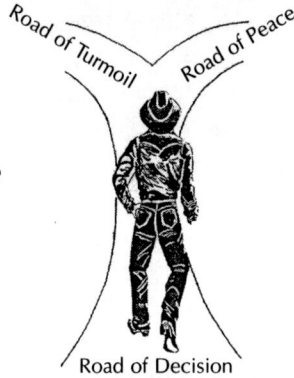

(How To
Make
Decisions)

Follow Peace

Hebrews 12:14 "Pursue peace with all people, and holiness,
without which no one will see the Lord." (NKJV)
Romans 8:14 "For all who are being led by the Spirit of God,
these are sons of God."

Jesus is the Prince of Peace and the fruit of the Holy Spirit includes peace. (Gal 6:22) The Holy Spirit leads, therefore, we are to follow Him.

Almost every week of my life, I give someone this advice - follow peace.

Sometimes when you are at a crossroad, you think to do something sometimes, you have a feeling down in your stomach not to do it. Actually it's down in your spirit in your innermost being. I call it "a check in your spirit." You may think "Oh, that's just me." It's not! It's the Holy Ghost saying, "No, no don't do it. There's trouble ahead." Now you can overlook "the check", but it always comes back. Problem is, when it comes back, it may be AFTER you have married the wrong person, took the wrong job, made the wrong move, got the wrong business partner, bought the wrong property, made the wrong business deal, took the wrong trip, and so on. Learn to hear from God. Follow that "check". What you are considering may look good, sound good, feel good. Everything says go for it, but you've got this check inside not to. You don't have peace about it. Follow peace! It's God trying to help you stay out of a mess.

On the other hand, it may look bad, sound bad and seem crazy. Everything and everybody says, "Don't do it." But you have peace about it, go for it. Be sure to pray and get the peace of God and the mind of God in it. Don't try to talk yourself into peace with your mind, will and emotions. That is your soulish area. Know down in your spirit.

Proverbs 3:6 "In all your ways acknowledge Him (God) and He will direct your paths." Jesus said, *"My sheep hear my voice and they follow Me..."* He is talking - we best be listening. Remember, the Lord always has your best interest at heart. He is wanting to keep us out of a wreck and lead you to a place of blessing.

Now, you can go in the peace and direction of God and still have battles, but He will take you through them. Moses didn't go over the Red Sea; he went through it with God. He saw a major miracle and experienced a wonderful victory for the nation of Israel. Paul, the apostle, was told by the Spirit of God to go to Rome. On the way there he had a shipwreck and was floating on a piece of wood to get to shore. However, he did make it to Rome.

Spend time in prayer. Spend time in the Word of God - the Bible. Be sensitive to the Holy Spirit. When you do what He says and go where He leads, it will always be in peace.

Jesus said in *John 14:27 "Peace I leave with you; My peace I give to you; not as the world gives, do I give to you. Let not your heart be troubled, nor let it be fearful."* and in *John 16:23* He said, *"These things have I spoken to you, that in Me you may have peace. In the world you have tribulation, but take courage; I have overcome the world."*

Another very important thing to remember is this. The

Bible says wisdom is the principle thing, so get wisdom and with wisdom get understanding (see Proverbs 4) How are we to do this? There are practical ways to check something out. But there is a supernatural way as well. Ask God for it. *James 1:5-6 "But if any of you lacks wisdom, let him ask of God, who gives to all men generously and without reproach (without finding fault), and it will be given to him. But let him ask in faith without doubting...verse 7 "For let not that man expect he will receive anything from the Lord.*

　　Psalm 46:10 "Be still and know that I am God..."

Wait on the Lord, be still before Him, get wisdom, get counsel, then go in peace. Many decisions we think need to be made now are not so urgent that you must decide immediately; you will have time to consider it in prayer and reading the Word until you get peace about it. But sometimes life puts out a situation that you must respond to immediately. That's okay. God is very capable of giving you quick direction and peace as to how to handle any and everything. Be quick to follow the check or the leading to go ahead from the Holy Spirit for a life of blessings.

　　Keep following Him. Keep pursuing peace.

PEACE WITH GOD: The first thing Jesus said to His disciples after He arose from the grave was "Peace be with you." (John 20:19) That is exactly what Jesus came to give us along with love, abundant life and life eternal. *Colossians 1:20 "and through Him to reconcile all things to Himself, having made peace through the blood of His cross;..."* If you don't have peace with God and know you are saved, pray this. "Lord, I am a sinner. I don't have peace with you. But right now I ask You to forgive me and wash me clean by the blood of Jesus. Thank You, Jesus, for dying for me on the cross and giving me a home in Heaven, peace on earth and peace with God. Holy Spirit lead me in peace and help me to be the child of God you want me to be. (Read John 3:16, Romans 3:10, 3:23, 5:8, 6:23, 10:9-10, 1 John 5:11-13) Now, get baptized, read the Bible everyday, pray everyday, and meet with other believers often.

Master Of Breakthroughs

7

Psalm 107:14
*He brought them out of darkness and the shadow of death, And
broke their chains in pieces.*

**1 CHRONICLES 14:8-11 Now when the Philistines heard that
David had been anointed king over all Israel, all the Philistines
went up to search for David. And David heard of it and went
out against them. (9) Then the Philistines went and made a raid
on the Valley of Rephaim. (10) And David inquired of God, saying, "Shall I go up against the Philistines? Will you deliver them
into my hand?" And the Lord said to him, "Go up, for I will
deliver them into your hand." (11) So they went up to Baal
Perazim, and David defeated them there. Then David said,
"God has broken through my enemies by my hand like a breakthrough of water." Therefore they called the name of that place
Baal Perazim. (Meaning Master of Breakthroughs).**

Notice above that David was anointed King and the enemy
came to search him out. When we are anointed by the Holy Spirit
to do a work for God the enemy will search us out and try to dis-
courage, change or stop the plan God has for our life. The anointing will destroy anything we come up against but we all will be
tempted, we all will have the opportunity to get discouraged.
None of us are exempt from trials. But the anointing will bring us

through to victory. (See Is. 10:27 and Romans 8:37)

Notice also David did not just jump up and go with out first consulting God. Good action. Always inquire of God and get the right battle plan. There are different battle plans for different battles as we will see. *Proverbs 3:6 "In all your ways acknowledge Him, and He will direct your paths."* Pray first - then go if that is what you should do.

Well God did tell David to go up against the Philistines and he defeated them, then he said, "God has broken through my enemies by my hand like a breathrough of water." When water breaks through a damn it takes out automobiles, houses, trees, bridges and roads. The Holy Spirit anointing gives us power. It's one thing to have a measure of the Spirit but it's another to have the Spirit without measure as Jesus said in *John 3:34 "For He whom God has sent speaks the words of God: for He gives the Spirit without measure."* Jesus also said in *John 7:38 "He who believes in Me, as the Scripture said 'From his innermost being will flow rivers of living water.'"* When you are baptized in the Holy Spirit you receive power to take the enemy out of the way. The Holy Spirit anointing takes out sickness, disease, bad attitudes, every assignment of the devil against your life. He can overcome every bondage a person is in. God is the Master of Breakthroughs. He can set you free from any addiction, from depression, from poverty or lack of finances, from a wrong relationship. He will breakthrough to get people out of hell and into heaven.

Let God have control, take His direction. God will bring you through but keep your guard up. A new battle may be brewing.

As we see in 1 Chron. 14:13-17 the Philistines came back to fight again. David inquired again of God. Remember there are different battle plans for different battles. This time God told David to wait. God Himself got closely involved and struck the enemy. So David just went in and cleaned up and finished the battle.

There are times when God will instruct us to just sit and wait. He will deal with others. We are to be led by the Holy Spirit and go in and finish when the timing is right.

So get your battle plan before you take off to do battle.

In the end David not only won the battles but the enemy feared him. Instead of walking in fear, our enemy, the devil, will be in fear and flee. *James4:7 Submit therefore to God.* Resist the devil and he will flee from you. And Deut. 38:7 says your enemy will come in one way and flee seven ways.

Daniel prayed 21 days before he got his breakthrough. (Daniel 10:12-13) Don't stop on day 20. Keep pressing in. Keep speaking faith words.

Psalm 107:14 says God broke their chains in pieces. What is chaining you? God will give you your breakthrough. Are you in bondage to fear, to pride, to jealousy, to tobacco in any form, to alcohol, to religious rules and systems, to unforgiveness, to sexual sin, to pornography, to homosexuality, to a lying spirit, to greed, to strife and rebellion, to sickness, to an old relationship, to the wrong job, to debt, to overeating, to junk foods, to some sin you feel like you cannot overcome. Jesus is the name above every name (Ephes. 1:20-21, Phil. 2:9) He has come to set you free. *John 8:31-32, 34 & 36 Jesus was therefore saying to those Jews who had believed Him. "If you abide in My word, then you are truly disciples of Mine; (32) and you shall know the truth and the truth shall make you free." (34) Jesus answered them, "Truly, truly, I say to you, everyone who commits sin is the slave of sin. (36) "If therefore the Son shall make you free, you shall be free indeed."*

If you have never repented of your sin you are in bondage to hell, to Satan, to the Kingdom of darkness. To repent means to change direction. Ask God to forgive you of your sin and submit to His will for your life and be willing to change in any area He asks you to.

God is the Master of Breakthroughs. He will break through to get you out of the Kingdom of darkness and into the Kingdom of light.

Ephesians 5:7-10 Therefore do not be partakers with them; (8) for you were formerly darkness, but now you are light in the Lord; walk as children of light (9) (for the fruit of the light consists in all goodness, righteousness and truth), (10) trying to learn what is pleasing to the Lord.

Jesus went to the cross to die for you, to take your sins on Himself so you could be forgiven and have eternal life and also abundant life here on earth.

BreakThrough to Heaven: Are you ready to break through and know your home is Heaven and eternal life is yours? Pray this. Dear God I am a sinner. I need a Savior. I need a break through. Forgive me of my sin, wash me clean. I accept Jesus right now as my Savior and Lord of my life. Thank You for dying for me on the cross to save me. I repent of my sins. Holy Spirit help me to live a new life and do what is pleasing to my Father in heaven. In Jesus Name I pray. Amen (Read Romans 3:10, 3:23, 5:8, 6:23, 10:9-10, John 3:16, Acts 2:38, 1 John 5:11-13) Read your Bible every day, pray everyday, get baptized, meet regularly with other believers.

Breakthrough from Bondage - Pray: Dear God I know you are the Master of Breakthroughs. I know Jesus came to set me free. I submit to you now. I need to be free in these areas of bondage and sin _____, _____(name them). I ask you to loose me now from every bondage, every assignment of the devil in my life, everything that is holding me back from being what you want me to be. And I thank you. I am free! In Jesus name. Amen.

8

The Holy Spirit Anointing "Upon" You

**You Can Have
God's Power
On Your Life**

*Acts 1:8 "but you shall receive power when the Holy Spirit
comes upon you;..."*

The Anointing of the Holy Spirit
Upon You for Power.
*Psalm 92:10 "But my horn (strength) You have exalted like a
wild ox; I have been anointed with fresh oil."*

What does anoint mean? To smear, to pour on, to rub with oil in order to set apart for a special work.

What is the anointing? It is the power of God. Let's stretch this out. It is the power of God in the earth today worked out in and through His people, by the Holy Ghost. (Holy Spirit or Holy Ghost is the same.)

Why do you need the anointing? *Isaiah 10:27 "It shall come to pass in that day that his (the enemy's) burden will be taken away from your shoulder, and his yoke from off your neck, and the yoke will be destroyed because of the anointing."*

Let's view other Scriptures where the word "**upon**" is used. In Acts 1:4 & 5 the disciples were told *"to wait for what the Father* *had promised, (5) for John baptized with water, but you shall be baptized with the Holy Spirit not many days from now."* Then in Acts 1:8 *"...but you shall receive power when the Holy Spirit has come **upon** you; and you shall be My witnesses in Jerusalem, and in all Judea and Samaria, and even to the remotest part of the earth."* John the Baptist said in *Mark 1:8 "I baptized with water but He (Jesus) will baptize with the Holy Spirit."*

When you are baptized (immersed) in or with the Holy Ghost you will receive power and boldness **upon** your life to be a witness for Jesus Christ, our Savior. Several things you will notice: (1) Boldness to witness (2) the gifts of the Holy Spirit will increase, see 1 Corinthians 12:8-10 (3) you will speak in tongues (4) more healings (5) signs, wonders and miracles will happen, see Acts 4:29-31 (6) More power against the devil (7) Prayer life will be more effective.

Jesus needed it. *Matthew 3:16 "And after being baptized, Jesus went up immediately from the water; and behold the heavens were opened, and He saw the Spirit of God descending as a dove, and coming **upon** Him.?"* If Jesus needed the power of the Holy Spirit **upon** Him, how much more do we need it? Notice, Jesus never did one miracle until after the Holy Spirit came upon Him for power. The Holy Spirit was already in Him because He was God's Son. The first thing Jesus did after the Holy Spirit came **upon** Him was to go out and defeat the devil in the temptation in the wilderness. When you are baptized in the Holy Ghost you will be a bold witness for Jesus and come against the devil, demons, sickness, disease, temptations and every assignment of the devil on your life.

It is one thing to have the Holy Spirit living in you. It's quite another to have the Holy Spirit **upon** you.

The best experience you will ever have in this lifetime is to receive Jesus as Savior and Lord. Your sins will be forgiven. Heaven will be your home. When you receive Jesus the Holy Spirit comes to live in you. The Holy Spirit also teaches you, is your Comforter, Helper, convicts you of sin, and raises you up to eternal life. *Romans 8:9 "...But if anyone does not have the Spirit of Christ, he does not belong to Him."* 1 Cor. 6:19-20 says our body is the temple of the Holy Spirit.

In the Old Testament stories we see what happened when the Spirit of God came **upon** people. David killed the giant Goliath; Gideon, with 300 men, defeated 135,000 men; Samson took the jawbone of an ass and killed 1,000 men; God performed extraordinary miracles through Elijah and Elisha. They all needed power to overcome the enemy. We need power also. We actually now have it better than those men. The Holy Spirit lives **in** us **and** can also be **upon** us.

It's one thing to have a measure of the Spirit, but Jesus said you can have the Spirit "without measure." John 3:34.

If you are saved and the Holy Spirit is in you, you can have another experience with the same Holy Spirit. Luke 11:13 says the Father will give the Holy Spirit if you ask.

In Acts 8:12, the people believed in Jesus and were baptized in water. So we know the Holy Spirit came to live in them but in verse 14, Peter and John heard about it and *vs. 15 "came down and prayed for them, that they might receive the Holy Spirit. (16) For He had not yet fallen **upon** any of them; they had simply been baptized in the name of the Lord Jesus. (17) Then they began laying hands on them, and they were receiving the Holy Spirit."* They had another experience with the same Holy Spirit. In verse 18 Simon saw it; what he saw was the people speaking in tongues because this happened in every account in Acts. *Acts 2:2-4 And suddenly there came from heaven a noise like a violent, rushing wind, and it filled the whole house where they were sitting. (3) And there appeared to them tongues as of fire distributing themselves, and they rested on each one of them. (4) And they were all filled with the Holy Spirit and began to speak with other tongues, as the Spirit was giving them utterance. Acts 10:43-48 "Of Him all the prophets bear witness that through His name every one who believes in Him receives forgiveness of sins." (44) While Peter was still speaking these words, the Holy Spirit fell upon all those who were listening to the message. (45) And all the circumcised believers who had come with Peter were amazed, because the gift of the*

27

*Holy Spirit had been poured out **upon** the Gentiles also. (46) For they were hearing them speaking with tongues and exalting God. Then Peter answered. (47) "Surely no one can refuse the water for these to be baptized who have received the Holy Spirit just as we did, can he?" (48) And he ordered them to be baptized in the name of Jesus Christ. Then they asked him to stay on for a few days. Acts 19:2-6 And he said to them, "Did you receive the Holy Spirit when you believed?" And they said to him, "No, we have not even heard whether there is a Holy Spirit." (3) And he said, "Into what then were you baptized?" And they said "Into John's baptism." (4) And Paul said, "John baptized with the baptism of repentance, telling the people to believe in Him who was coming after him, that is, in Jesus (5) And when they heard this, they were baptized in the name of the Lord Jesus. (6) And when Paul had laid his hands **upon** them, and they began speaking with tongues and prophesying.*

In Acts 10:42-48 "the Holy Spirit fell **upon** all who were listening" to Peter and in (vs 46) "For they were hearing them speak with tongues and exalting God", then (vs 48) they were water baptized.

You will find out in 1 Corinthians 12 and 14 that there is "speaking" in tongues to be interpreted for the whole assembly to be edified (built up) and also there is "praying" and "singing" in tongues which builds you up so you can go out to build others up.

Jesus was anointed with power to do good and heal. (See Acts 10:38) When He came to earth He left the power of God there. He needed that power on earth and received it. We need the same power. The Holy Spirit comes **upon** you, fills you to overfilling then from your innermost being comes power.

To receive eternal life: Pray this. Lord I am a sinner, I need a Savior. Forgive me of my sin. I accept what Jesus did on the cross when He died and shed His blood for me. I receive Jesus now as my Lord and Savior. I turn from my sin to you. I receive eternal life. I now call God, my Father. Holy Spirit, help me to live a life pleasing to God. In Jesus name I pray. Now get water baptized, read your Bible everyday and meet with other Christians to grow in Christ.

Receive the Holy Spirit: The Holy Spirit can fall **upon** you as you listen to the message of Jesus; Spirit filled believers can lay hands **on** you and pray, or you can pray to be filled with the Holy Ghost according to Luke 11:13. Pray this. "Father, as your child I ask Jesus to baptize me in the Holy Spirit with power and I receive it now." As you begin to pray words other than your natural language will begin to come out. You will be praying from your spirit to His Spirit, from your innermost being. You will be a bold witness for Jesus. Also see Romans 8:26; Ephesians 5:18 and Jude 20-21.

This chapter was inspired from the book
"When the Holy Spirit Comes Upon You"
by Glenn Smith - Rodeo Cowboy Ministries.

Baptism In The Holy Spirit
The Holy Spirit lives in you when you receive Jesus as Savior and Lord
- The Holy Spirit come upon you for power.
Note: Holy Spirit or Holy Ghost is the same.

Mark 1:8 and Luke 3:16 Jesus will baptize you in the Holy Ghost and fire.
Matthew 3:16 and John 1:32-33 The Holy Spirit descended and remained **upon** Jesus.
Acts 1:5 ...You shall be baptized with the Holy Spirit....
Acts 1:8 But you shall receive power when the Holy Spirit comes **upon** you; and you shall be My witnesses...
Acts 2:1-4 Day of Pentecost- they were all filled with the Holy Spirit & spoke in tongues as the Spirit gave them utterance.
Acts 4:29-31 healing, signs, wonders, miracles, speak boldly.
Acts 8:12, 14-17 Believed in Jesus, baptized in water, hands were laid on them - Holy Ghost came **upon** them.
Acts 10:44-48 Holy Spirit fell **upon** them as Peter spoke of Jesus and they spoke in tongues and prophesied.
Acts 19:1-7 Paul laid hands on them, the Holy Spirit came on them -

they spoke in tongues and prophesied.

Romans 8:26 the Holy Spirit intercedes for and with you with groanings too deep for words.

Jude 20-21 build yourselves up; praying in the Holy Spirit keeping yourselves in the love of God.

Luke 11:9-13 ask God for the Holy Spirit.

Pray: Ask Jesus to baptize you in the Holy Ghost with the evidence of speaking and praying in other tongues & for power to be a witness for Jesus Christ and to be an overcomer and walk in victory.

Water Baptism
baptize-from the Greek word baptizo meaning - "to immerse"

Matthew 3:13-17, Mark 1:9-11, Luke 3:31-22 Jesus' Baptism.

John 3:22-23 Baptized where there was much water.

Matthew 28:19 Go and make disciples of all nations - baptizing them...

Mark 16:15-16 Go into all the world.

Acts 2:38 Repent and be baptized.

Acts 8:12 (Philip in Samaria) When they believed about the kingdom of God and the name of Jesus, they were baptized both men and women alike.

Acts 8:25-34, 35-38 Ethiopian eunuch believed; was baptized.

Acts 22:16 Why do you delay? Arise and be baptized...

Acts 10:43-46, 47-48 Gentiles receive Holy Spirit and are baptized.

Acts 16:14-15 Lydia in Macedonia. She and her household are baptized.

Acts 16:23-24 Philippian Jailer. He and his household having believed, were baptized.

Romans 6:4 Therefore, we have been buried with Him through baptism into death so that as Christ was raised from the dead to the glory of the Father we too might walk in newness of life.

*Note: In the Bible people were baptized only **after** they received Jesus as Savior and Lord.*

The Ministry Of Angels

Angels Are Sent Out To Help You

Psalm 34:7 The angel of the Lord encamps all around those who fear Him, and delivers them.

The Ministry Of Angels
Hebrews 1:14 "Are they (angels) not all ministering spirits, sent out to render service for the sake of those who will inherit salvation?"

Angels are sent to render or give service, to serve those who have received Jesus as their Savior, because they are the ones who will inherit salvation or eternal life. So as a "believer' you can "expect" help from angels. You can dispatch angels to help you. Angels are here to help the children of God plus a lot more.

The ministry of angels includes the following (and more):
• **1. Angels deliver God's message** - Example: The angel Gabriel spoke to Mary that while she was a virgin she would conceive a baby by the Holy Ghost, give birth to our Savior, and to name Him Jesus. (Luke 1:26-35) Also, an angel announced the birth of Jesus Christ to the shepherds in the field outside Jerusalem. (Luke 2:7-14)

• **2. Protection** - II Kings 6:6-23 tells a story of the Syrian army surrounding Elisha and his servant. His servant was overtaken in fear but Elisha saw a great number of angels. See *verse 6 "So he answered, 'Do not fear, for those who are with us are more than those who are with them.'"* He prayed and God opened the eyes of his servant to see the mountain full of angels. The angels struck the whole Syrian army blind and Elisha led them to be taken captive by the King of Israel.

• **3. Worshipping God** - Rev. 5:11-12 Thousands of thousands of angels worship God in heaven.

• **4. Angels have and will proclaim the gospel (the good news of Jesus)** - *Rev. 14:6-7* tells of an *"angel flying in midheaven, having an eternal gospel to preach to those who live on the earth,..."*

• **5. To serve and minister to our needs** - even food, clothing, healing, finances, rescue, safety, finding lost articles, such as mail, etc. and getting them to you.

• **6. To help the church and the Kingdom of God here on earth** - Angels proclaim God's message, protect His people, fight battles, deliver messages from God, and undergird the work of Jesus who is the Head of the church.

• **7. Angels deliver us out of trouble** - In Acts 12:1-11 an angel led Peter out of prison to safety.

• AND ANGELS DO EVEN MORE •

More about protection and deliverance:

Psalm 91:11 "For He gives His angels charge over you, to keep you in all your ways. (12) In their hands they shall bear you up, lest you dash your foot against a stone."

Psalm 34:7 "The angel of the Lord encamps all around those who fear Him, and delivers them."

There is a lot of talk about angels today. We see a lot of angel pins and artifacts. Remember they are not good luck charms. God does not even deal in luck, rather He pours out blessings.

WARNING: We are not to worship angels. *Rev. 19:9-10 "...And I fell at his feet to worship him. And he said to me, 'Do not*

do that; I am a fellow servant of yours and your brethren who hold the testimony of Jesus; worship God...'"
Beware of counterfeits. II Cor. 11:14-15 shows that Satan disguises himself as an angel of light and so do his servants. Col. 2:18 shows that the fallen angels who now serve Satan could try to give you ungodly visions. So how do you know if an angel is in fact from God? They will never deliver a message or do anything contrary to God's Word. *Gal. 1:6-8 (8) "But even though we, or an angel from heaven should preach to you a gospel contrary to that which we have preached to you, let him be accursed."* They will not contradict the Bible.

Back to the ministry of angels. As I began seeing all that the angels do for us, I got excited and realized this - God has given us so much to make it through and succeed in life. He has given us His Word - the Bible, Jesus and the Name of Jesus, The Blood of Jesus with the work of the cross, the Holy Spirit, friends to encourage and help us, angels, and even Himself as our Father.

Today, we pray for angels to encamp about us, protect us, our families, animals, houses and possessions.

The men in a town in Mexico several years ago were going to run a missionary lady out of town but fear gripped them and they would not go close to her house when they saw the "big men" outside - They were angels.

In the six days war with Israel in 1967 the Turks left their tanks in the field and ran. Later they asked, "Who were those big men who were dressed in white?" - They were angels.

Lately during my quiet time of Bible study and prayer I have dispatched angels to keep the mosquitoes off of me. I didn't see the angels but the mosquitoes didn't bite.

A partner in this ministry figured if the angels could do that for me, they could give him some wind to cool him off as he built fence on a hot, sunny day. He said, "okay boys, start flapping them wings." He got his breeze.

I read a book by a well known evangelist and prophet who dispatches angels to bring in finances when his ministry is in need. Remember - angels serve God, serve His children and point us to

Jesus.

Those who will inherit salvation: This is who angels help. Will you inherit salvation? Will you go to heaven when you die? You can. Pray this and mean it from your heart. Dear God, I am a sinner, separated from You. I am sorry for my sins and I ask you to forgive me. I accept Jesus now as my Savior and the Lord of my life. Thank you Jesus for dying for me on the cross so I can have a home in heaven and live forever with You. Help me Holy spirit to live a life pleasing to God, my Father. In Jesus Name I pray.

The Law Of First Things

1ST
GOES TO
GOD!

You Need To Understand This -
This Gets God Involved In Your Life

*Proverbs 3:9 & 10 "Honor the Lord with your possessions,
and with the first fruits of all your increase;
(10) so your barns will be filled with plenty, and your vats will
overflow with new wine."*

God requires **first** place in our lives to be able to bless us. There is no other place He can occupy. If you have ten sheep you may think you should give God the best one, but He doesn't require the best one, He requires the **first**born. When you give God the first of your increase, you are saying, "God you have **first** place in my life." Then you are in a position for Him to bless you.

Mat. 6:33 *"But seek **first** the Kingdom of God and His righteousness, and all these things shall be added to you."* The Kingdom of God is "God's way of doing things". Let's see what is God's way of doing things.

We can enjoy the benefits of the Law of **First** Things. So let's get understanding on this principle.

See *Exodus 34:19, 20, 26 (19) "All that open the womb are Mine, and every male **first** born among your livestock, whether ox or sheep. (20) But the **first**born of a donkey you shall redeem with a lamb. And if you will not redeem him, then you shall break his* *neck. All the **first**born of your sons you shall redeem. And none shall appear before Me empty handed. (26) The first of the **first**fruits of your land you shall bring to the house of the Lord..."*

This is one of the greatest "keys to blessings" you will find. There is a reason God requires your **first**fruits. It is so He can bless you, it shows where your heart is and where your priorities are. God desires to open the windows of heaven and pour out blessings onto your life.

We need to understand three terms **(1) Lord (2) redeem (3) first.**

(1) Lord "there is none above." Jesus is Lord. He is the Master, the Boss, He holds the highest position in our life.

(2) redeem - to buy back by replacing with an acceptable sacrifice.

(3) first - means exactly that - **1st.** God demands **1st** place in our lives.

We see in Ex. 34 above that the firstborn belong to God. It was sacrificed to God if it was a clean animal. God declared the following to be clean animals - oxen, sheep, goat, pigeons, turtle doves. If it was an unclean animal it had to be redeemed (or replaced) with a clean animal. This is why He said to give a lamb in place of the donkey. If this was not done the donkey's neck was broken. A live donkey would seem to give us more use than a dead donkey; but blessings in doing things God's way far outweighs the perceived value of keeping something that is to be given to God. God knew we would move from an agriculture system of giving to a money system. It works the same way. Give God the first of your increase.

When you give to God the **first**fruits of your increase - it establishes what place He is in your life. It establishes Lordship. **You see, giving to the Lord first - It's not about money - It's about Lordship! It's about putting God 1st.**

The two areas we are challenged in the most is our time and our money. Are you going to start your day by giving God first place by reading His Word, the Bible, and praying or is it jump and go to make some more coins in your pockets? Are you going to give God the first of the increase in your money or will you put the money to your own use? Remember when you give **first** to God - it takes the curse off the rest and puts a blessing on.

See Ezekiel 44:30 "The best (first) of all **first**fruits of any kind, and every sacrifice of any kind from all your sacrifices, shall be the priest's; also you shall give to the priest the first of your ground meal, to cause a blessing to rest on your house."

Another term we must understand is **tithe. Tithe means 10%.** Paying the tithe was established by Abraham in Genesis before the Law was given by Moses. The tithe is holy to the Lord. The tithe still belongs to God's work. Actually, the tithe, the 10% should always be paid **first** off the top of your increase. By doing this the rest of what you have is redeemed - the curse is taken off and the blessings are put on. In Malachi 3:6-12 The people wanted to return to God and His instructions were to bring the tithes and offerings to Him. Why? Because it showed what place He was in their life. It had to be #1. **It's not about money - it's about Lordship.** He said He promised to open the windows of Heaven and give them more than enough to fight their battles against the enemy with them and to bless them so much that others would see and say they were blessed.

In Deut. 26:1-15 the people were instructed to bring Him their **first**fruits and when they did, it put them in a position to ask for and expect to receive blessings. They basically said "God we have obeyed, we have given the tithe, the **first**fruits, so look down from heaven and bless us." This is the tither's prayer (Read it in verses 14-15)

The Law of **First** Things can be seen many places in the Bible. In Genesis, Abel and Cain gave an offering to God. Abel's was accepted, Cain's was not. Abel gave the "firstborn" of His lambs but Cain gave "out of some" of the crops. So Abel not only offered a blood sacrifice, but the firstborn. He was saying that God was first place in his life.

God operates under His own law. He gave His **first**born, Jesus, to redeem us. He took the curse off all mankind and put the blessings on. He is the Lamb of God who takes away the sin of the world. (John 1:29) "He is the only one who could buy us back from sin and hell. He is the only "acceptable sacrifice." Jesus is the one who gives us Heaven and eternal life instead of the curse of hell and separation from God. It's up to us to receive Him as Savior and Lord. It's up to us to receive what He did for us.

Jesus is the "acceptable sacrifice." He redeemed you. Have your received Him? *John 1:12 "But as many as received Him, to them He gave the right to become the children of God, even to those who believe in His name."* To receive eternal life pray this. "Dear God I am a sinner I ask your forgiveness. I need a Savior. I receive Jesus right now into my life to be my Lord. You are now **#1** in my life. Help me to always put You first and do things Your way. In Jesus name I pray. Amen."

Giving first fruits: God gave His Son, the firstborn to enlarge Heaven. When we receive Jesus we take on the nature and love of God. We desire to give firstfruits offerings to enlarge Heaven, to win souls to His Kingdom. You see it's not about money - it's about Lordship, it's about your heart, it's about souls, it's about putting God **1st**. We receive help in this ministry from **first**fruits money, time, prayers and helps. We pray for and expect blessings on those who give.

This chapter was inspired by the book *"When God Is First"* by Mike Hayes pastor of Covenant Church in Plano, Texas.

What To Do In The Valley

Change The Name Of Your Valley

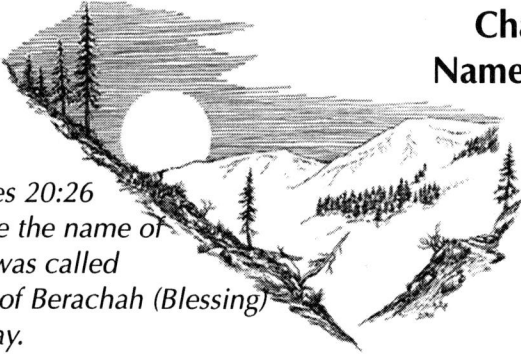

II Chronicles 20:26
...; therefore the name of
that place was called
The Valley of Berachah (Blessing)
until this day.

Psalm 23:4 Yea, though I walk through the valley of the shadow of death, I will fear no evil; for you are with me: Your rod and your staff, they comfort me.

I. THE VALLEY OF THE SHADOW OF DEATH (Psalm 23:4)

Three things we need to remember in the valley: **Number 1 - It's just a "shadow"** - of death-not death - shadows don't hurt, they just feel like it, they put fear in us only if we let them; don't fear them.

Number 2 -" Through" - We all go through seasons; we all have our valley times. Don't stop in the middle of the mess. Keep going through. Moses led Israel through the Red Sea, not over or around but through. God brought them through and He will do so for you to.

When it looks like you are dying, your business, your career, is dying - often you are going through the shadow of death not death! So keep your eyes on Jesus, the author, perfector, and finisher of your faith. (Heb. 12:2)

Number 3 - "For you are with me". God is with you even when you feel alone. Recently God stirred Psalm 23:4 to my mind - I said, "God that's all I need to know. If you are with me everything is going to be okay."

One year a steer wrestler was about to call it quits in his steer wrestling career, it looked dead. His dad encouraged him, he practiced some more and went on do become the World Champion Steer Wrestler.

Seventeen years ago the Lord gave me this Scripture when my son, Caleb, became sick and as a one day old baby his lungs closed down due to Group B strep. The Lord spoke Psalm 23:4 to me. I thought, "He is not going through death - just the shadow of death." After fighting the good fight of faith for 32 days he made it home, out of the hospital and has lived a healthy life.

In August 2001 I was injured in a rodeo in the bareback riding event. I was in the shadow of death. My intestine was burst open and I was bleeding internally from a ruptured artery. But it was only a shadow. I never had any fear, only pain. Today I am healthy with no related problems.

II. VALLEY OF REPHAIM (GIANTS) (I Chronicles 14:8-17)

David changed the name of this valley from giants to Baal Perazim meaning **"Master of Breakthroughs."** The Philistines came to fight King David and all Israel in IChronicles 14:8-17. David did a wise thing. He asked God if he should go up against them and God said, "Go up for I will deliver them into your hands." David defeated them and changed the name of the valley from giants to Master of Breatkthroughs because God broke through the enemies "like a breakthrough of water;" like a flood. But the enemy came back for more battle. David did not just go do as before. No, he wisely inquired of the Lord again. God gave him a different battle plan. God Himself took care of the enemy and wiped most of them out and David went in and drove the rest back. Then the enemy and all the nations around feared him.

Remember there are different battle plans for different battles. Seek God. How do I handle this battle Lord? Wait for the answer, then do as He leads you and change the name of your valley to breakthrough.

III. VALLEY OF BERACHAH (BLESSINGS) (IIChronicles 20:1-30)

In IIChronicles 20:1-30 three nations came against King Jehoshaphat and the nation of Judah. (vs 2) Fear set in (vs 3) Jeshosophat set himself to seek the Lord. He remembered God's promises and who God really is (vs 6-12) Focus on the promises not the problems. He did not know what to do. Maybe that is where you are today. Jehoshaphat prayed in *vs. 12 "...For we have no power against this great multitude that is coming against us; nor do we know what to do, but our eyes are upon You."* God answered in *vs. 15 "Do not be afraid nor dismayed because of this great multitude, for the battle is not yours, but God's"* The people began to praise God and faith arose (vs 19-20) Then Jehoshaphat sent the praise singers out before the army as they marched into battle (vs 21). This is an important **key to victory** - Begin to praise God before you see the victory. Praise confused the enemy, they fought among themselves and killed each other. (vs 22-23) Praise will cause demonic activity coming against us to cease. It took Israel three days gathering the spoil off the dead bodies because there was so much valuables and precious jewelry. What began as a valley of certain defeat, curse and death became a blessing. On the fourth day they assembled and the name of that place was called the Valley of Berachah which means Blessing until this day. Trust God - your valley can become a blessing.

IV.   VALLEY OF DECISION (Joel 3:14)

Joel 3:14 "Multitudes, multitudes in the valley of decision! For the day of the Lord is near in the valley of decision." This is about the end of the world. Jesus came, lived among us, died for us to go to heaven. You must decide to receive Jesus to have eternal life. *"He who believes in the Son (Jesus) has eternal life; but he who does not obey the Son shall not see life, but the wrath of God abides on him." John 3:36.* It's your decision.

V. VALLEY OF DEATH (I Corinthians 15)

Jesus went to this valley for me and for you. It was not just a shadow. It was death and yet He lives. The Bible teaches us in Romans 8:11 that "The same Spirit that raised Jesus from the dead will raise our mortal bodies." Jesus went through death and took the sting of death away for us who love Him. *ICor. 15:54 says "Death is swallowed up in victory (55) O Death Where Is Your Victory? O Death Where Is Your Sting?"* There is no sting in death for us who know Jesus and have eternal life. *(vs 57) "But thanks be to God who gives us the victory through our Lord Jesus Christ."*

FROM THE VALLEY OF DEATH TO LIFE - The Bible declares that all have sinned and fall short of the glory of God and that we are dead in our sins. But there is a way to life. Jesus said in *John 14:6 "I am the way, and the truth and the life; no one comes to the Father, but through Me."* He came to bring us to the Father, to deliver us from death and hell to life and heaven. If you want this pray, "God I am a sinner, I need a Savior. Forgive my sins. I receive Jesus as my Savior right now and I thank your for dying on the cross to save me. Thank you for getting me out of this valley of death and for giving me eternal life. Help me to live a life pleasing to my Father in heaven. In Jesus Name, Amen. (Now read Romans 3:10, 3:23, 5:8, 6:23, 10:9-10, 13, John 3:16, Acts 2:38) Read the Bible everyday, pray everyday, get baptized, meet with other believers often).

    One way to walk in the valley of blessings is to be a giver. Help ministries and churches get people out of their valleys back to the mountaintop. God declares *"Give and it shall be given unto you..." Luke 6:38.* It is a Bible principle. Giving leads to blessings.

12

Having Done All "Stand"

The mind of Christ--Faith, Believing God, Health, Abundance, Joy, and Love

Fear
Lack
Troubles
Strife

Worry, Doubt, Unbelief, Sickness

(When Healing Is Not Instant)
Ephesians 6:13

Ephesians 6:13 - Wherefore take unto you the whole armor of God, that ye may be able to withstand in the evil day, and <u>having done all, to stand.</u> (KJV)

We must learn to stand by faith on the word of God even when everything around us seems to be falling apart and nothing seems to be going right and our prayers don't get the quick response we feel we so desperately need. I had to stand firm on the word of God in a serious situation and put to work what I preach. We must **learn** the Word, **keep** the Word, **believe** the Word, **speak** the Word and **act** on the Word. The Word of God has all the keys to victory you and I will ever need.

My sixth child was born on May 6, 1989. A Group B Strep

germ attacked him in the birth canal causing his lungs to close down. Also, pneumonia set in. He was taken by ambulance to a hospital where one doctor worked on him for 12 hours. Then it was on to University Children's Hospital in Houston, Texas by Life Flight Helicopter. He was in intensive care for 23 days, most of the time being on a respirator or breathing machine, plus 9 more days in special care. The first specialists that talked to me about his condition said, "What we have in there is a hand grenade and the pin is already pulled." It was time for spiritual warfare.

Our new son didn't have a name until he got sick. I said, "We've got to name him Caleb because in the Bible (Numbers 13:30), Caleb said, "we are well able to overcome it," and I believed God would help our Caleb overcome too. His full name is Caleb Joseph Christian (and he is a fighter). In the natural he was one breath away from death - he turned purple twice and had CPR for 15 minutes one time - but in the spiritual realm, God had given me many, many promises and keys to victory from His word. The doctors were great, the nurses super, but I'm sure that it was the word of God and faith in it that kept Caleb alive. (They told us that Group B Strep is the worst sickness they have to fight in newborn babies in ICU at the hospital).

I needed a "rhema" - a word or words from God. Many of you may be going through tough times. Ask God for a rhema, a special word from God for your particular situation. Begin to read his word, the Bible, and a Scripture or Scriptures will become more real to you than whatever your situation is as the Holy Spirit will show you just what you need. See "Keys to Victory" below. These may help you too or you may need to find other Scripture for your situation.

I told Caleb although he was out on medication, "We're going to get our oxygen. We're going to get our miracle." And God, by His grace, honored those words. *Isaiah 54:13-17 says "great shall be the peace of thy children;"* God has a way to destroy the enemy that comes against us and *"no weapon formed against us shall prosper."*

A special verse I told the nurses and others was *Psalms*

112:1-2, 7. (1) Blessed is the man who fears the Lord and delights greatly in his commandments. (2) His seed shall be mighty on earth. (7) He is not afraid of evil tidings. His heart is fixed, trusting in the Lord. These and other Scriptures became more real to me than what I could see, feel, taste, smell, or hear. Praise God for His Word.

My sincere thanks to all of you who spent much time in intercessory prayer for Caleb. Caleb is now a strong healthy young boy.

Look up the Scriptures for better understanding and apply them to your situation. *Joshua 8:26 shows us that we are to stay in battle until the enemy is utterly destroyed, until victory is complete.*

Sometimes the battles are over soon. I took my son, Kyle, to the hospital emergency room when he was only a few months of age. He was very weak. They were about to do a spinal tap. I leaned over to talk to him and healing scriptures came out of my mouth. The lady doctor walked over; I told her what I had done, then she took a light out and Kyle began to follow the light and focus on us. They stopped the process and did not do the spinal tap. We took him home. She said, "Take him home." The next day she said, "The lab people say there is something in his blood but I don't think they are right. Take him home again." The next day the doctor said that the blood work was normal and whatever it was was gone.

Speaking of the word of God - *Acts 4:12 lets us know there is salvation in no one else other than Jesus.* If you haven't settled the issue about your eternal destiny, now would be a good time. Ask God to forgive your sins and turn away from them. Believe in Jesus as your Savior and Lord and you will be saved. See Romans 3:23, 5:8, 6:23 and 10:9-10. Also 1 John 5:11-13 and Rev. 3:20.

Keys To Victory

Mark 16:17-18. They shall lay hands on the sick and they shall recover.

John 10:10. The thief comes only to steal, and kill, and destroy: I (Jesus) came that they might have life, and might have it abundantly.

Ephes. 1:21. Jesus is the name above every name (above sickness, distress and every evil).

Matthew 18:18. Whatever you shall bind on earth shall be bound in heaven; and whatever you loose on earth shall be loosed in heaven.

Matthew 18:19. Prayers of agreement. "...if two of you agree on earth about anything that they may ask, it shall be done by My Father who is in heaven."

Proverbs 4:20-22. The word of God - is life to those who find it and health to all their flesh.

Psalm 107:19. Cry unto God in your trouble and He will save you from your distresses.

Psalm 107:20. "He sent His word and healed them, and delivered them from their destructions."

Psalm 107:21. Praise the Lord for goodness (and thank Him before you see the victory. Also see Psalm 67).

Isaiah 54:13-17. No weapon formed against us shall prosper.

II Cor. 10:3-5. The weapons of our warfare are mighty through God to pull down strong holds. Cast down imaginations that are not from God;... Think the thoughts of Christ. (KJV)

Deut. 28:1, 4, 7, 11. Hearken diligently unto God - your children, your produce, your cattle and all will be blessed;...the enemy will flee.

Romans 10:17. Your faith will build as you hear (and read) the word of God.

Revelations 12:11. We have overcome the devil by the word of our testimony and the blood of the Lamb (Jesus). (Note: Plead the blood of Jesus over your family. There is power in the blood.)

Psalm 23:4. Fear no evil, even if death is very close. (Also John 14:27.)

Psalm 139:23-24. Ask God to show you your sins and ask forgiveness so your prayers won't be hindered. Isaiah 59:2 says our iniquities separate us from God.

Matthew 6:14-15. Forgive everyone who has harmed you or sinned against you.

Psalm 112:1-2, 7. Our seed shall be mighty on earth. Don't' be afraid of evil tidings, fix your heart, trusting God.

James 4:7. Resist the devil and he will flee - Draw near to God, and He will draw near to you.

Mark 11:22-24. Have faith in God. Speak to your mountain (or situation), don't doubt but believe. God will give to you whatsoever you say. (Note: Be careful about words of confession; they are very important and powerful.)

Psalm 91:11. God has sent angels to protect us.

Ephesians 3:20. God is able to do above all that you ask or think.

Matthew 6:10. Determine that God's will will be done in your life.

John 14:13 and **John 16:23.** Pray in the name of Jesus.

Romans 8:26. Pray in the spirit when you don't know what to pray.

Joshua 8:26. Stay in your battle until the enemy is utterly destroyed; until your victory is complete.

Read the above verses and those that precede and follow them for a fuller understanding.

Continue to believe for instant healings.

Remember, God still heals instantly. But if you do not get your miracle immediately or at least soon, keep believing the Word of God - stay in your battle until you get victory. By faith believe for a good report. You get what you believe for - so **Believe for a good report!**

Also remember: *Exodus 15:26 "...for I am the Lord that healeth thee." Exodus 23:25 "And ye shall serve the Lord your God and He shall bless thy bread, and thy water; and I will take sickness away from the midst of thee."* (KJ)

Matthew 8:17 "...He Himself took our infirmities, and carried away our diseases." (see Isaiah 53:4)

1 Peter 2:24 "...by His wounds (stripes) you were healed.

Don't Limit God

*Psalm 78:40-41 "How often they provoked (rebelled against)
Him in the wilderness, and grieved Him in the desert
(41) Yes, again and again they tempted God,
and limited the Holy One of Israel."*

The Israelites that Moses led out of slavery kept testing God, trying Him, murmuring against Moses and God, and walked in doubt and unbelief. This put a limit on the very blessings God was desiring to bring to them. They complained that there was no water, no food, and that Moses had led them there to die and be put in graves. But God gave them water, food, kept them alive and fulfilled His promise to get Israel into the promised land.
DON'T LIMIT GOD!
- Don't Limit God
- Don't despise the day of small things (beginnings)
- Don't trust in riches
- Don't trust in your own power and might
- Don't forget to thank God after your blessing comes

DON'T FORGET TO THANK GOD AFTER YOUR BLESSING COMES - *Luke 17:11-14* In this story Jesus cleansed 10 lepers. *Verse 15 says "Now one of them, when he saw that he had been healed, turned back, glorifying God in a loud voice, (16) and he fell on his face at His feet, giving thanks to Him." (17) And Jesus* answered and said 'Were there not ten cleansed? But the nine-where are they?'" The one got an even greater blessing. See *vs.* 19 *"And He said to him, 'Rise, and go your way; your faith has made you well'"* (Also this has been interpreted "your faith has saved you.") The nine were made well physically. This one was made whole physically and spiritually. The nine were saved from sickness, the one was saved from sickness and sin. His body and his heart were cleansed.

DON'T TRUST IN YOUR OWN POWER AND MIGHT - *Deut. 8:11-19* This is somewhat like the other story above. God was bringing His people to the land of abundance. Success was coming. Yet to get it all, they had to work at it, to walk it out, to do battle, to defeat the enemy. But it was God who supplied them their plans and their strength to get the job done. *Verse 11-18 says (11) "Beware that you do not forget the Lord your God by not keeping His commandments,..."* When you have eaten and are full, when you have silver, gold, cattle, when you defeat the enemy, He desires us to stay humble or else we will say as in *vs.* 17 *"then you say in your heart 'My power and the might of my hand have gained me this wealth.' (18) And you shall remember the Lord your God for it is He who gives you power to get wealth, that He may establish His covenant which He swore to your fathers, as it is this day."*

Keep practicing, studying, working hard at what you do. When you become successful remember it is God who supplies you what you need. Remember God! Give Him thanks!

DON'T TRUST IN RICHES - *I Tim. 6:17 "Instruct those who are rich in the present world not to be conceited or to fix their hope on the uncertainty of riches, but on God, who richly supplies us with all things to enjoy."* Remember the man in the Bible who became rich? He said to himself that he would build bigger barns and store up enough to last many years. He was trusting in his riches but his riches could not keep him alive. God required his soul that very night as he planned his retirement. Trust in God - not your riches.

DON'T DESPISE THE DAY OF SMALL BEGINNINGS - Sometimes the size of your business, how much you have won (as in rodeos), your business, your church, your ministry or how you see yourself as small compared to your peers, can cause others or even yourself to despise your beginnings. But God lets us know if we are faithful in a little, He can trust us with much. Be faithful where you are now and you will be able to handle increase better when it comes. Keep walking by faith.

Zechariah 4:6-12 Remember *"'not by might nor by power, but by My Spirit' says the Lord of hosts."* It is by God's power you will do your accomplishments and achieve your dreams. Zerubbabel was to build the temple. The beginning work seemed so small. But God said in *vs. 10 "For who has despised the day of small things?"* He goes on to say that they would see the plumb line in the hand of Zerubbabel. The plumb line was to check the straightness of the wall. In other words the wall, the job, would be complete. He started small and finished big. You can too. Do not despise your size. Just keep growing.

DON'T LIMIT GOD

1.) We limit God by saying, "I can't" when He says, "We can."

2.) We limit God when we don't walk by faith. *II Cor. 5:7 for we walk by faith, not by sight* - Walking by what we see, feel, taste, touch, hear and smell can limit God.

3) Walking by circumstances limit God - Circumstances can change but the Word of God never changes. The Word is what changes your circumstances. Read the Bible - get a Word from God about your circumstances - they will change.

4) Don't limit God in prayer. *Mark 11:24*

5) Don't limit God with what you say. *Mark 11:23*

6) Don't limit God when you are sick. *James 5:14-15*

7) Don't limit God when you lay hands on people.

  • Lay hands on the sick - they will recover. *Mark 16:18*
  • Lay hands on people for blessings
  • Lay hands on people for the baptism in the Holy Spirit
  • Lay hands on people to send them out for ministry and on mission trips.

50

EXPECT MIRACLES! - **DON'T LIMIT GOD TO THE STORIES IN THE BIBLE** -We are a people of God today. He still heals, fills, delivers, helps us and provides our needs. *Hebrews 13:8 "Jesus Christ is the same yesterday and today, yes and forever."*
DON'T LIMIT GOD IN WHO HE CAN FORGIVE AND SAVE - *Romans 10:13 "for 'Whoever will call on the name of the Lord will be saved.'"* He can save your boss, your spouse, your children, hateful people, even people who say there is no God. He can also save youand give you eternal life. If this is your desire pray this. "God I am calling on you now. I confess I am a sinner. I ask you to forgive me of my sin. Thank you Jesus for dying on the cross for me to wash me clean. I ask you to be my Savior and I receive you now as Lord of my life. I am now your child, saved from hell on my way to You in Heaven. Holy Spirit teach me how to live a life pleasing to God. In Jesus Name I pray, Amen." Now read your Bible everyday, pray everyday, and meet with other believers regularly to grow in Christ. Get a church home. *(See Rom. 3:10, 3:23, 5:8, 6:23, 10:8-10, John 3:16, Acts 2:38)*
DON'T LIMIT GOD IN YOUR GIVING - The Bible declares over and over *"give and it shall be given to you."* As you give - it is called seed and *"God gives seed to the sower"* II Cor 9:10. As you give firstfruits and the first 10% of your increase-the tithe and special offerings, God will supply your needs and more so you can seed again. We speak blessings on you.

Fresh Oil!

Psalm 92:10 "...I have been anointed with fresh oil."

Fresh Oil
Psalm 92:10 "But my horn (strength) You have exalted like a wild ox; I have been anointed with fresh oil."

Oil is a symbol of the Holy Spirit. It represents God's presence and power in your life. Oil was poured on priests and kings to set them apart for the work they were called to do. They were anointed. To anoint is to rub in, smear, or pour on. The power of God would come on them and they would go out and do mighty works for God.

Many people today have experienced the presence and power of God. They have seen Satan defeated in many areas of many lives. But for some reason - apathy, lack of excitement about Jesus, failure to grow in Christ, getting satisfied with yesterday's victories, or whatever else - they are not experiencing the power of God today. They live in yesterday's victories when God is saying *"They are new every morning"* (Lamentations 3:23). We need to learn to drink daily from God's Word, the Bible, pray daily, be sensitive to the Holy Spirit, stay teachable, receive correction and continually be filled with the Holy Spirit.

On the day of Pentecost in Acts 2 the disciples (about 120 in all) were baptized in the Holy Spirit and fire. They not only began to speak in tongues as the Spirit gave them utterance but immediately went to the streets and about 3,000 souls were won to Jesus that very day. Peter knew he could not live on yesterday's glory so in Acts 4:29-31 he prayed to be filled again for boldness to continue to be effective for the Kingdom of God. *Acts 4:29 "And now, Lord, take note of their threats, and grant that Thy bondservants may speak Thy word with all confidence (boldness) (30) while Thou dost extend Thy hand to heal, and signs and wonders take place through the name of Thy holy servant Jesus (31) And when they had prayed, the place where they had gathered together was shaken, and they were all filled with the Holy Spirit and began to speak the Word of God with boldness."*

You don't necessarily need a new "Word" from God or a new Scripture - you need a **fresh Word**. *"For the word of God is living and active..." (Heb. 4:12).* Jesus said, *"the words I speak to you are spirit and are life" (John 6:63).* Pray for fresh oil, fresh anointing. Pray that the Bible will come alive to you, even in Scriptures you have known for a long time. When the Word of God is fresh, it will produce the desired results - salvation, healings, deliverance, peace, and victories. Remember - *"...the yoke will be destroyed because of the anointing oil."* (Is. 10:27 in the New King James version - because of the anointing in KJV).

You see in Acts 2, Peter had an experience with the Holy Ghost. In Acts 4, he had another experience with the same Holy Ghost. There is one baptism in the Holy Ghost but many fillings. Perhaps you need a fresh filling today for today's battles and challenges.

A lady came to a Cowboy Church - Bandera meeting. She told us she had been close to God at one time but now she felt so far away. She was ready to come back. I told her, *"draw near to God and He will draw near to you."* Through tears of repentance and joy she said, "That's the first Scripture I learned sixteen years ago." She knew it was James 4:8 but that night it became fresh in her spirit again, produced joy and a knowing that she was accept-

ed by God. She knew she was still loved by God and also by those
of us who were there. You see, she did not need a new Word, she
needed a **fresh Word** - fresh oil. She left refreshed that night.

God wants us to continue to produce fruit for the kingdom
of God. *Psalm 92:14 "They shall still bear fruit in old age; they
shall be fresh (full of oil or sap) and flourishing (green)."*
Something green is alive and still producing.

FOR FRESH ANOINTING - If you feel dried up, almost
lifeless concerning the things of God although you have experienced His power in the past pray this, "Father I need fresh oil, a
fresh anointing from You. Fill me fresh with the Holy Spirit so I can
be effective to serve you all the days of my life. Make Your word
come alive in me again. I ask for fresh, fresh, fresh oil. I receive
it and I thank You. In Jesus name, Amen.

THE FIRST STEP TO FRESH OIL - When you receive Jesus
as Savior, the Holy Spirit comes to live in you and will raise you to
eternal life. This first experience with Jesus is essential for eternal
life and is your first experience with the oil of the Holy Spirit which
gives you love, joy and peace and power to live a life pleasing to
God. If you are sorry for your sins and ready to turn from sin and
receive Jesus, Pray this. "Dear God I am a sinner. Forgive me. I
need a Savior. I receive Jesus as my Savior now and I make Him
the Lord of my life. Thank you for dying on the cross for me and
giving me eternal life. Fill me with the oil of the Holy Spirit and
give me power to be the child of God You want me to be. Fill me
fresh everyday. In Jesus name I pray."

Now (1) Get baptized (2) Read the Bible everyday (3) Pray
everyday (4) Meet with other Christians regularly (5) Tell others
about Jesus. (See Romans 3:10, 3:23, 5:8, 6:23, 10:9 & 10 and
John 3:16 and 1 John 5:11-13.

Also you can have a spirit filled believer anoint you with
oil and/or just pray for you to receive a fresh anointing and fresh
oil from the Holy Spirit. As they lay hands on you and pray for
you, breath it in and receive it.

The Wind Of Change

Ecclesiastes 3:1 To every thing there is a season, a time for every purpose under heaven.

The Wind Of Change
Isaiah 43:19 "Behold, I will do a new thing, now it shall spring forth; Shall you not know it? I will even make a road in the wilderness and rivers in the desert."

Life is always changing. I've noticed so much change in people and their circumstances lately. You're happy - then you're sad, healthy - then you're sick - then healed to enjoy healthiness again, you have a job - you don't have a job, you're satisfied - then you're not, you're single - then you're married, you're lost - then you're saved, you're hot for God - then you're lukewarm, you're poor - then you have plenty, finances are great - then you suffer lack, you have clear direction in life - then you seem to lose your purpose, and sometimes all is well but you feel a stirring inside that a change is coming.

With all these changes and more, I'm reminded of how important it is to constantly be led by the Holy Spirit and to continue to daily ask God for wisdom.

Romans 8:14 "For all who are being led by the Spirit of God, these are the sons of God."

James 1:5 "But if any of you lacks wisdom, let him ask of God, who gives to all men generously and without reproach (without finding fault), and it will be given to him."

It is important to stay in touch, tuned in to the voice of the Holy Spirit. Develop a hearing ear as you read the Word of God and pray. Spend time listening to Him.

Different battles require different battle plans.

What you have done in the past may not work in the present. King David would often go to God for his battle plans. In *2 Samuel 5:17-25* the Philistines attacked Israel two times. David inquired of the Lord, saying *"Shall I go up against the Philistines?"* The Lord told him to *"Go up, for I will doubtless deliver the Philistines into your hand."* The Philistines were defeated, but then they came again against Israel. David inquired of the Lord about what to do. This time God said, "You shall not go up." He told David not to go up but circle around behind them, wait until he heard the sound of marching in the tops of the mulberry trees, and then to advance quickly. Then the Lord went out before him to strike the Philistines. David did as the Lord commanded and drove the enemy out.

What can we learn from this? Seek God's plan with each new battle, new challenge, new change. There's a time to respond immediately, there's time to wait then go. Go in God's timing and God will do mighty things for you and in you.

Let's talk about change in four ways.

(1) Some things are not changing because you are not changing.

We must be willing to change. I've heard that the "definition of insanity" is "to keep doing what you have always done and expect a different result." Also - "If you keep doing what you have always done - you will keep getting what you have always gotten."

Jesus said, "Repent." The word repent means a change of heart, change of mind, change of direction. If you are living a life apart from God, repent. Be sorry enough for your sin to change.

(2) Change is constantly taking place.

Continue to draw near to God and He will draw near to you. (James 4:8) and *Proverbs 3:6 "In all your ways acknowledge God and He will direct your paths."* As stated above - Continue to be led by the Holy Ghost and seek wisdom from God.

(3) Some things will change, like it or not.

Learn to hear God, get an answer on what to do and how to handle it, how to adjust, or how to change with the change. God will bring you through in peace in every change.

(4) Learn to change things by God's Word.

Get the Word in your heart and in your mouth. It will make a difference now and for eternity.

Romans 10:8-10 But what does it say? "The Word is near you, in your mouth and in your heart" - that is the word of faith which we are preaching, (9) that if you confess with your mouth Jesus as Lord, and believe in your heart that God raised Him from the dead, you shall be saved; (10) for with the heart man believes resulting in righteousness, and with the mouth he confesses, resulting in salvation."

This settles your eternity. This is a major change. Your direction was hell, now it's changed to Heaven.

Some things won't change until you speak the Word out of your mouth. Speak to your mountains! Learn what the Word says about your situation and speak it out. *Mark 11:23 "Truly I say to you, whoever says to this mountain, 'Be taken up and cast into the sea,' and does not doubt in his heart, but believes that what he says is going to happen it shall be granted him.'* (or in the King James version of the Bible, *"he shall have whatsoever he saith."*) There is a time to pray and a time to say.

In *Acts 3:6-8, Peter spoke to a lame beggar, "'In the name of Jesus Christ the Nazarene, walk'* ... and immediately the lame man stood and began walking and leaping and praising God."

In *John 20:22 Jesus breathed on His disciples and said,*

"Receive the Holy Spirit." When you receive Jesus, the Holy Spirit comes to live in you giving eternal life. *John 3:8 "The wind blows where it wishes and you hear the sound of it, but do not know where it comes from or where it is going; so is everyone who is born of the Spirit."*

THE BIG CHANGE: The biggest change comes when you give control of your life to God. When you go from hell to heaven, when you turn from self and the devil to Jesus. When you repent (or change) from sin to right living and right standing before God. The Bible says, *"You must be born again."* (John 3:7) and in *John 3:3* Jesus said, *"Truly, truly, I say to you, unless one is born again, he cannot see the Kingdom of God."* To be born again is to be born from above or born of God. If this is your desire say "I am a sinner. I need a Savior. I want to change. Forgive me God. I receive Jesus now as my Savior and Lord of my life. Thank you for saving me and for dying for me on the cross. Thank you for changing me so I can go live forever with you. Holy Spirit help me to change anything that does not please my Father in Heaven. Guide me and give me wisdom. In Jesus name, Amen.

EXPECT CHANGE: When you pray and/or speak to your mountains (sickness, situations, temptations, attitude, problems) expect by faith for God to move in your behalf and change things for the good. *Psalm 62:5 says "...my expectation (hope) is from Him."* (KJ)

All Your Needs Are Met

Friends

Good Job

Good
Health

Peace
of Mind

Philippians 4:19 "And my God shall supply all your needs according to His riches in glory in Christ Jesus."

Every need you ever needed was taken care of at the cross. I wrote a teaching once entitled "Benefits For You At The Cross." I told the story of how my son, Caleb, as a newborn baby (1989) was in intensive care and how he turned purple and the doctors did CPR on him to keep him breathing and alive. The doctor who came out to tell me what was happening was also a Catholic nun. I said, "You just be Sister Katherine for a minute." Then I took her by the hand and prayed, "Father, when your Son, Jesus, went to the cross, He took care of every need we ever needed and I thank you for it." Then I told her, "Now you go back in there and do your thing and I will do mine." I continued to pray and believe God for a good report. In a short time the emergency situation was over. He is now a healthy young teenage boy.

Everything Adam gave away in the Garden of Eden, Jesus won it back. He supplies all your needs - spiritually, physically, emotionally, financially, socially and provides direction for your life.

In only part of Luke 5 we see Jesus meet all of these needs. Peter was a fisherman. He spent the whole night fishing and caught nothing. He did what Jesus said to do - he let the net out again and caught so many fish that his nets were breaking. Fishing was his livelihood so now his "financial needs" were met. (see vs.

4-9) Then Peter left everything and followed Jesus. His "direction" and focus on life had now changed. Instead of catching fish, he went out to catch men for God by bringing them to the Savior, Jesus. (see vs. 10-11)

Then (in vs. 12-13) a man with leprosy came to Jesus asking to be cleaned. Jesus said, *(vs13) "...I am willing, be cleansed."* And immediately the leprosy left him. Jesus is still willing, He is still the healer. Know Jesus as your healer. The "physical needs" were met and also his "social needs", and "emotional needs". He had been an outcast as a leper. He could now live among his family, friends and society again.

Next Jesus went off to pray, as we should, to refill and get refreshed. Spend time with the Lord to get continued direction and the mind of God on our course of life.

Next in (vs. 18-25), some men brought a paralyzed man on a bed to Jesus; they let him down through the roof because they could not find a way through the crowd. *(vs 20) "And seeing their faith,"* He said, *'Friend, your sins are forgiven you.'"* Then Jesus said, *(vs 24) "...rise and take up your stretcher and go home."* At once he rose, he took up what he had been lying on and went home. His "physical needs" were met and his "spiritual needs" were also met. His sins were forgiven.

Next *(in vs 27-28) Jesus told Matthew, the tax-gatherer, "Follow Me."* And he left everything behind to follow Him. His "direction" and purpose in life changed.

The emotional needs were met for all of the above people. Gloom and doom, debt, sickness, depression, life without purpose and direction were now turned into a good report and joy in the Lord.

The gospel is Good News. In Mark 1:14 & 15 Jesus came preaching the gospel.
• It's good news that if we are sick - Jesus is the healer.
• It's good news that if we are in turmoil - Jesus is our peace.
• It's good news that if we are in sin - we can be forgiven.
• It's good news that we don't have to go to hell.
• It's good news that Jesus made a way for us to go to heaven.

• It's good news that Jesus heals the brokenhearted & broken dreams.

• It's good news if we are in need of finances - God is our provider.

• It's good news that all of our needs are met in Christ Jesus.

• It's good news that we can pray to God for protection and direction. He heals our bodies, our minds, our spirits, our hearts, our animals. We have seen God heal people, horses, cats and dogs. He meets our needs!

That is what this teaching is all about. Let's go back to *Philippians 4:19 "And my God shall supply all your needs according to His riches in glory in Christ Jesus."* Who was the Apostle Paul talking to here? It was those who were giving into his ministry. They had given more than once for Paul's needs. Paul had some needs. In *Phil. 4:10* he said he rejoiced that *"you have revived your concern for me."* But in vs 11 & 12 Paul said that he had learned the secret of being content when he was filled and when he was hungry, with having an abundance and suffering need. Then Paul said the often quoted *Phil. 4:13 "I can do all things through Christ who strengthens me."* He goes on to share the blessings of a giver. To the Philippians from Macedonia he said *(vs 15) "...no church shared in the matter of giving and receiving but you alone; (16) for even in Thessalonica you sent a gift more than once for my needs."*

Now this is the key we need to know. They were givers. They met Paul's personal and ministry needs. This put them in a position to receive. Then Paul said in *vs. 17 "Not that I seek the gift itself, but I seek for the profit which increases to your account."* Paul knew the promises and nature and principles of God. Give and it shall be given. In blessing you will be blesssed. Get a hold of this - it will change your life. Be a giver - God will see to it that you will also be a receiver as He blesses you back.

Remember it was because of their giving that God promised *Phil. 4:19 "And my God shall supply all your needs according to His riches in glory in Christ Jesus."*

The Greatest Need. God knew that we were sinners and needed a Savior. He sent His Son Jesus to take our sins in His body on the cross and die for us so we could have eternal life. Our greatest need was forgiveness and to stay out of hell and go to heaven. If you want to receive eternal life through Jesus, pray this. "God I am a sinner, I need a Savior. Forgive my sins. I accept what Jesus did for me on the cross. I believe Jesus is the Son of God and that you raised Him from the dead to give me eternal life. Jesus, be my Savior now. I confess that Jesus is Lord. I receive eternal life now and a home in heaven with You. Holy Spirit help me to live a life pleasing to my Father in heaven. Thank you for meeting my greatest need and all of my needs. In Jesus name I pray. Amen. (Now read Romans 3:10; 3:23; 5:8, 6:23; 10:9-10, John 3:16) Get baptized, read your Bible, pray everyday, and meet with other believers often.

Jesus Today!

Presenting Jesus
- He Still Cares -

Hebrews 13:8 "Jesus Christ is the same yesterday and today, yes, and forever."

Jesus Christ is Lord of today. He is not a God of yesterday only, not just a God of the past. He is the same, His character is the same, His attributes are the same, His power is the same. He is still the miracle worker and guide and friend and deliverer and Savior we need for today's world.

Don't relegate or restrict Jesus to some historical figure that lived in the past, in a period of time on the earth, who did miracles, got involved in people's lives and died and that was the end of His power. No, He was raised from the dead and is seated at the right hand of the Father and He said just before parting his disciples *"...and lo, I am with you always, even to the end of the age."* (Matt. 28:20) Don't think Jesus did miracles only in "the Bible days' - **these are the Bible days!** Jesus is the same.

Since He is the same as yesterday, let's see what He was like yesterday so we can know what He is like today. *Matthew 4:23-25 "And Jesus was going about in all Galilee, teaching in their synagogues, and proclaiming the gospel of the kingdom, and healing every kind of disease and every kind of sickness among the people. (24) And the news about Him went into all Syria; and they brought to Him all who were ill, taken with various diseases and pains, demoniacs, epileptics, paralytics; and He healed them. (25)*

And great multitudes followed Him..."

Matthew 9:35-38 *And Jesus was going about all the cities and the villages, teaching in the synagogues, and proclaiming the gospel of the kingdom, and healing every kind of disease and every kind of sickness (36) Then He said to His disciples, "The harvest is plentiful, but the workers are few. (38) Therefore beseech the Lord of the harvest to send out workers into His harvest."* Then in Matt. 10:1 He gave authority to His disciples over unclean spirits, to heal every kind of disease and in *verse 7* to preach saying, *"The kingdom of heaven is at hand."*

The above describes what kind of Jesus walked the earth and He is still the same today. Also He is the same forever. He knows we need a Shepherd, a Father in heaven, a Savior for eternity. So He continues to send out workers to preach the gospel and perform signs, wonders and miracles, to heal broken bodies, broken hearts, broken dreams, to give peace of mind, do away with confusion, to let people know He is not mad at them, He wants to help them, to save them and set them free from anything holding them back from being God's best. He is still moved with compassion. He still takes away fear and puts in trust and courage. He forgives sin. He takes away bitterness and hate and gives love.

Jesus healed the multitudes, He healed Peter's mother in-law of fever, raised Jairus' daughter from the dead, healed the woman who had an issue of blood for 12 years, helped Peter's finances with a boat load catch of fish, caused the lame to walk and blind to see, healed people emotionally and spiritually. Then He sent His disciples, that's you and me after we receive Him, to do the same. (see John 14:12)

Jesus of today is your Helper, your Healer, your baptizer in the Holy Ghost. He will baptize (immerse) you in the Holy Spirit for power to live the Christian life, heal the sick, rebuke the devil, be a bold witness of who Jesus is and lead people to repentance of sins and faith in God and eternal life through the Savior, Jesus Christ.

Examples of Jesus of today. We have seen God do wonderful things in this ministry at rodeos, cowboy churches and other places. We have seen Jesus heal lumps in breasts, bone problems and fear in horses, M.S. and other painful diseases, torn muscles strengthened and pain gone among other things as well as people receiving Jesus.

Jesus is the same forever! Our bodies and minds can be healed but it is your spirit that will live forever. He came to give us eternal life. A bareback rider told me once just before he was to ride that he always saw me passing out the magazines (The Christian Cowboy Magazine). He said, "I thought maybe I ought to read one." He did. He was wearing a cross. I said, "It sounds like you got Jesus in your head, you need to get Him into your heart." We prayed right then and before he got on to ride he asked Jesus to be his Savior and Lord, to come into his heart. He got on his horse and rode as a born again, Jesus loving believer." Jesus still loves those who call on His name.

Get Jesus involved in your situation today! Pray, invite Him in. He is a God of today. He loves to help-it's His nature.

Jesus Today - If you don't know this Jesus who can give you love, joy, peace, healing, victory and eternal life, you can today. Pray this. "Dear God, I am a sinner, I need a Savior, I ask you to forgive me and today I invite Jesus into my heart and life to be my Savior and Lord. Thank you for dying on the cross for me so I can have eternal life in heaven and thank you for caring about me in today's world. I invite you to be with me in all that comes my way. Now today I am saved and God is now my Father. *Romans 10:13 "for whoever will call upon the name of the Lord will be saved."* Read the Bible and pray daily, get baptized and meet with other believers often.

What Can We Do Today? The followers of Jesus in yesterday times supported the work of the ministry and were cheerful and at times were sacrificial givers. *II Cor. 9:7 says, "God loves a cheerful giver"* and *verse 10 says "He gives seed to the sower."* So today you can give and sow seeds of prayer, helps and finances for this ministry to help us keep preaching Jesus today and everyday.

chapter 18 — Continue In The Things Of God

Winners never quit...

II Timothy 3:14 You, however **continue** *in the things you have learned and become convinced of, knowing from whom you have learned them; (15) and that from childhood you have known the sacred writings which are able to give you the wisdom that leads to salvation through faith which is in Christ Jesus.*

Are things seeming to crumble right before your eyes? Does it seem like things have gone from good to bad - then bad to worse? There are a lot of obstacles to face - not just face but to **overcome** in life. I exhort you to **continue** in the faith of our Lord Jesus Christ. Fight the good fight of faith. (I Timothy 6:12) Don't bend, don't bow and don't break. "Fixing your eyes on Jesus, the author and perfector (or finisher) of our faith, who for the joy set before Him endured the cross, despising the shame, and has set down at the right hand of the throne of God." (Hebrews 12:2) Verse 1 just before this tells us to lay aside every encumbrance, and the sin which so easily entangles us, and let us **run with endurance** the race that is set before us. So **continue!** Don't quit, don't weaken. We are in this life to persevere and win through God's mercy, help, love and grace.

Look at our prime example, Jesus, in the above Scriptures.

He was **determined to continue** in the course God laid out for Him. We are the joy that was set before Him. He had to die on that cross for us to be reconciled to God. It is the shed blood of Jesus that cleanses us from our sin (I John 1:7). It sure wasn't any fun. But our Lord Jesus had the "spirit of a finisher." He prayed in *Luke 22:42 saying, "Father, if thou art willing remove this cup from Me; nevertheless not My will, but Thine, be done."* Praise God, Jesus continued on to the cross at Calvary. Now, by receiving Him as Lord and Savior we don't have to go to hell, separated from God; we can be in heaven and live forever with God, our Father.

Paul, the apostle, knew what it meant to **continue** in spite of his circumstances. (Philippians 4:11-13) Remember, your circumstances are subject to change, but the word of God is not. God is on our side when we love and serve him and are yielded to do His will. You may still have some battles, but **you can go through them** with God's help. *Philippians 4:11 "Not that I speak from want; for I have learned to be content in whatever circumstance I am. (12) I know how to get along in humble means, and I also know how to live in prosperity; in any and every circumstance I have learned the secret of being filled and going hungry, both of having abundance and suffering need. (13) I can do all things through Christ who strengthens me."* Paul **determined to continue** in his love and faith in God and look what happened - vs 18 - says he had an abundance. Why? Because not only did he continue to serve the Lord but also the faithful people in the church at Philippi continued to give into his ministry and the work of the Lord. And then they too were blessed because they **continued to give**. They were told in *Philippians 4:19, "And my God shall supply all your needs according to His riches in glory in Christ Jesus. (20) Now to our God and Father be the glory forever and ever. "* Amen.

So if you're having problems **continue to trust God.** Resist the devil and he will flee. Draw near to God and He will draw near to you . (James 4:7-8) I Peter 5:8-10 tells us to resist the devil, then **after you have suffered** for a little while, the God of all grace through Christ will himself perfect, confirm, strengthen and establish you.

Back to II Timothy 3:1-6 at the start of this article. It sounds like today's news reports. "Men will become lovers of self, lovers of money, boastful, arrogant, revilers, disobedient to parents, ungrateful, unholy, unloving, irreconcilable, malicious gossips, without self-control, brutal, haters of good, treacherous, reckless, conceited, **lovers of pleasure rather than lovers of God...**" It goes on to say evil men will proceed from bad to worse. And then verse 14 tells Timothy in that atmosphere of events - continue in the things of God.

II Timothy 3:16 *"All Scripture is inspired by God and profitable for teaching, for reproof, for correction, for training in righteousness; (17) that the man of God may be a adequate, equipped for every good work."*

God has equipped you to win. He has given you the keys to victory. **He loves you, Continue** in His Word. Do what He wants you to do. Be what He wants you to be. **Continue!!**

Knowing The Father - He wants you to become a child of His. You must accept Jesus to receive a spirit of adoption as sons by which we cry out, "Abba! Father!" (Romans 8:15) You can know you have eternal life. *I John 5:12 "He who was the Son (Jesus) has the life; he who does not have the Son does not have the life. (13) These things I have written to you who believe in the name of the Son of God, in order that you may know that you have eternal life."* If you've never received Jesus as your Savior, God is not your Father. If you've never confessed your sins and have not been forgiven of your sins you are not on your way to heaven. Stop right now if your desire is to change all that and pray from your heart. "Dear God I confess I am a sinner and separated from you. I ask you to forgive me of my sins. Cleanse me by the blood of Jesus. Dear Jesus, thank you for dying on the cross for me while I was still a sinner. I accept you now as my Lord and Savior. I receive eternal life right now through my faith in You and I give you praise for saving me and giving me a home in heaven. Help me to continue in life to do the things that are pleasing in your sight. In Jesus name I pray. Amen.

Persistence

Luke 11:8 I tell you, even though he will not get up and give him anything because he is his friend, yet because of his persistence he will get up and give him as much as he needs.

The above verse is the end of a parable, a story about a man wo wakes his friend up at night to get some food for another friend of his who has come on a journey to visit him. The story is from Luke 11:5-8 and the teaching on it continues in verses 9-13. The teaching is also in the book of Matthew. *Matthew 7:7 "Ask and it shall be given to you; seek and you shall find; knock and it shall be opened to you. (8) For everyone who asks receives and he who seeks finds, and to him who knocks it shall be opened. (9) Or what man is there among you, when his son shall ask him for a loaf, will he give him a stone? (10) Or if he shall ask for a fish, he will not give him a snake, will he? (11) If you then, being evil, know how to give good gifts to your children, how much more shall your Father who is in heaven give what is good to those who ask Him!"* (See also Luke 11:9-13) *Luke 11:13 "If you then, being evil, know how to give good gifts to your children, how much more shall your heavenly Father give the Holy Spirit to those who ask Him?"*

You may say, "I've done that." Well, keep on asking, keep on seeking and keep on knocking.

In Mark 2:1-13, friends brought a paralytic to Jesus to be

healed. They couldn't get in the door of the house so they let him down through a hole they made in the roof. They had **Persistence.** They were not giving up until they got what they came for. The result: *vs 5 "And Jesus seeing their faith said to the paralytic, 'My son, your sins are forgiven.' vs 11 'I say to you, rise and take up your pallet and go home' (12) And he rose and immediately took up his pallet and went out in the sight of all;..."* Thank God for friends that will help and persevere with you in prayer and help you out, friends who won't give up, but will join their faith and **persistence** with yours.

And look at Bartimeus, a blind man who received his sight when he came to Jesus. Mark 10:46-52 *(vs 47) "And when he heard that it was Jesus the Nazarene, he began to cry out and say, 'Jesus, Son of David, have mercy on me!'" 48 And many were sternly telling him to be quiet, but he kept crying out all the more, 'Son of David, have mercy on me!'* Maybe you have been crying out to God for a long time. People around you have told you to be quiet about it, stop asking God, quit all that believing, all of that confession, all of that praising and praying. Well look at Bartimeus. He had **persistence.** He cried out **all the more.** The result; *vs 49 "Jesus stopped and said, 'Call him here.' vs 51 And answering him, Jesus said, 'What do you want me to do for you?' And the blind man said to Him, 'Rabboni, (my Master), I want to regain my sight!' vs 52 And Jesus said to him, 'Go your way; your faith has made you well.'* And immediately he regained his sight and began following him on the road." He got his healing quickly but **it was his persistence that got Jesus' attention.** So He asked the man, "What do you want?" He wants for us to tell Him what we want, what we need, even though He already knows before we ask. The Holy Spirit will teach us how to pray about our situations but we still need to ask, then believe and thank God for the supply or answer and receive it.

Many of you have trained barrel racing horses to become winners through sheer **persistence;** horses that could run but wouldn't turn. You went around those barrels enough times, over and over, until finally you had a winner on your hands. Your **per-**

od calf roping horses. Many
rain **but through persistence**
wboys have less natural ath-
of persistence to reach their
buckles and saddles.
quitting. Your biggest bless-
ming soon. *Hebrews 10:35*
onfidence, which has a great
durance (or patience) so that
I, you may receive what was
e who shrink back to destruc-
the preserving of the soul."

is the same yesterday, and
or you as he did for the para-
, many that came to Him and
are still coming to Him.   Be persistent." Get to Jesus. Cry out all
the more. Keep asking, seeking and knocking. God will move on
your behalf as He sees your faith.

And don't forget Jesus is also knocking; knocking at your
hearts door. Won't you let Him come in?

Persistence to Heaven: Revelation 3:20 "Behold, I stand at
the door and knock; if anyone hears My voice and opens the door,
I will come in to him and will dine with him and he with Me." Be
persistent enought to finish what you know God wants you to do.
He wants you to have eternal life with Him in Heaven. Accept
Jesus as Savior and Lord; open the door of your heart and life right
now. Confess that you are a sinner and ask God to forgive you of
all your sins and thank Him for doing it right now. Get baptized,
pray every day, read the Bible every day, fellowship (meet) with
other believers regularly. If you have any questions about this and
your soul's destiny, **read** Romans 3:10, 3:23, 5:8, 6:23, 10:9-10
and John 3:3-8, John 3:16 and Mark 16:15-16 and I John 5:11-13.
If you are a Christian already but have not turned everything over
to the Lord, open all the doors to your heart and life and let Jesus
take charge and be Lord of all. Pray and do it right now.

Out Of Bondage - Into Freedom

John 8:31 Jesus said, "If you abide in My word, then you are truly disciples of Mine: (32) and you shall know the truth and the truth shall make you free." (34) "...Truly, truly, I say to you, everyone who commits sin is the slave of sin." (36) "If therefore the Son shall make you free, you shall be free indeed."

God's desire and design is for us to experience an abundant life and to enjoy the trip. Now to do this we must abide in His word - do things His way, not our own. *Is. 1:19 "If you are willing and obedient, you shall eat the good of the land. (21) But if you refuse and rebel, you shall be devoured by the sword."*

There is a fallacy in the church thinking which teaches that "When you get saved everything is suddenly okay." It's not okay! We are forgiven - yes. We are saved - yes. We have eternal life - yes. But we also have consequences from present actions and sometimes from the past to deal with. We have a mind that needs to be renewed to God's way of thinking and acting. (See Romans 12:1-2). Also we have iniquities which come through our own repeated sins and actions and from generational curses. There are strongholds in your life that need to be broken and put to an end.

Let me ask you. **Are you tired of hearing about the wonderful Christian life with the love and joy only to find yourself and your family not living it out for very long at a time?** You seem to keep coming back around to a place of strife, hurts, frustration, unforgiveness, division, bitterness, fear and a sinful lifestyle. You know Jesus gives us love, joy and peace. But somehow you are missing it.

Well let's close the door on the devil! Let's root out things or should we say let's get to the root of the problem that blocks our blessings, the thing that causes curses and cut it out of our life.

Remember - if there is a curse, there is a cause. *Proverbs 26:2 "...a curse without a cause does not come." ["...a curse causeless does not come."* (KJ Version)]

Notice the Bible talks of sin, transgression and iniquity. Sin is missing the mark. It's when you don't do what God says or you do what He says not to. You don't give it much thought, you just sin. Transgression is more rebellious. You know it is wrong, you think about it but you decide to step into it anyway.

Iniquity becomes a part of you. Iniquity is being "twisted" in your thinking and behavior. Iniquity is a "bentness toward." Iniquity comes through generational curses or habitual sin. Ask God to show you the iniquity in your own life. Pray to God to reveal it, then confess it and ask God to remove it from you and from your family. If you are a parent of young children take your authority as a believer and in Jesus Name say, "It stops here. This iniquity (name it) is broken off me and my children by the Blood of Jesus."

If there is any sin in your life - even a bad attitude confess it, repent, ask God to forgive you and remove any evil spirits which influence you in that area of your life. *Matthew 6 says "deliver us from evil."* Get serious about this part of the prayer Jesus taught His disciples.

Those of us in the body of Christ must **deal with unforgive-ness.** Unforgiveness will wreck your life. Forgiveness is a must. **Choose to forgive** and your feelings will catch up later. When Jesus taught His disciples to pray He said in *Mat. 6:12, "forgive us our debts as we forgive our debtors."* See Mat. 6:14-15 and *Mark 11:26 "But if you do not forgive, neither will your Father who is in heaven forgive your transgressions."* You are a slave to the one you do not forgive. It is sin. Jesus came to set you free from sin so do it now. Say, "I forgive (name them) by an act of my will. I release them to You, God, vengeance is Yours not mine. Forgive me now Lord. In Jesus Name. Amen." Also hurt from others can cause a wound. If you have a wounded spirit, tell God, He will heal you. Say, "God I have a wounded spirit and heart but Jesus came to heal the broken hearted." By speaking it out of your mouth it is brought out of darkness to light. God will take the pain and heal the wound. (You may remember the details but it won't hurt anymore. In time you won't even think about the details).

Another way we fail to have joy is by the devil's intrusion. Satan comes in by legal ground as we sin and act in such a way he is allowed access to us. But Satan also comes in through intrusion. When this happens do this *James 4:7 "Submit to God. Resist the devil and he will flee from you.(8) Draw near to God and He will draw near to you..."* Say as Jesus said, "Get thee behind me, Satan." Or maybe just "Hit the road. Be gone."

Also if you have gone through emotional trauma such as a divorce, death of someone close to you, loss of something or someone special to you, a spirit of heaviness can come on you. Mourning is always for a short season with God then He picks you up and brings you laughter, joy and strength again. Sadness, heaviness and depression is real but we are not to live our lives in that condition continually. The Bible says to *"put on a garment of praise for a spirit of heaviness."* As you begin to sing praise and worship songs the spirit of heaviness will go. It's like a splinter in the finger - when the splinter is removed; the pain goes. When Moses died the people of Israel wept for 30 days then they went on. The Holy Spirit wants you to go on. His joy and help will take you out of depression back to joy and enjoyment of life.

The spirit of fear among other things can keep you from the abundant life of Jesus. Remember, when the spirit goes, the fear goes. God did not give us a spirit of fear, but of power and love and a sound mind. (II Tim. 1:7) If God did not give you the spirit of fear; it must come from the devil. So say, "You foul spirit of fear go in Jesus Name. You must go. I receive only the Spirit of God which gives me boldness and confidence and a sure hope for the now and for my future. I submit to God; devil, you must flee. Also every lying spirit and spirit of error must go. In Jesus Name, Amen."

I SPEAK LIFE AND FREEDOM: "I speak life to each of you reading and needing this and call every assignment of the devil out of your life along with every evil spirit. Loose the people! I call you into freedom! In Jesus Name."

FREE FROM HELL: We need to be set free from eternal death more than anything else. Jesus came to give eternal life. Romans 6:23 "For the wages of sin is death, but the free gift of God is eternal life through Christ Jesus our Lord." Pray this. "God I am a sinner. I need a Savior. Forgive me. Thank you for sending Your Son, Jesus, to die for me on the cross to shed His blood to wash away my sins. I receive Jesus Christ as my Savior and Lord right now. I walk out of bondage to sin and hell and I walk in freedom and forgiveness and Your love now. Jesus is Lord. Heaven is now my home. Holy Spirit help me to live a life that is pleasing to my Father in heaven. Help me to stay free!! In Jesus name, Amen. Read Romans 3:23; 10:9-10, Acts 2:38. Read the Bible and pray daily.

You can be free from allergies, asthma, cancer and lingering sickness which is in your family's history. You can walk free from rebellion, horoscopes, ouija boards, witchcraft; also from fear, worry, inferiority or fear of man, woman, authority, failure or success. You can walk free from addictions; also from pride, gossip, judgementalness. You can be free from alcohol, cigarettes, bulimia, anorexia, drugs, adultery, fornication, pornography, also from homosexuality, twisted thinking and gender confusion; plus from suppressing ministries and causing church splits and giving up on Christianity. We can walk free from ongoing accidents, grinding teeth, suicidal thoughts; also from depression, despair, discouragement, loneliness and having a wounded spirit; also from lying, deception, bad self-image. You can go free from jealousy, anger, divorce, hatred, revenge and from error, confusion, irresponsibility and inappropriate thinking and behavior. You can be set free from constant fatigue, procrastination and having your success blocked. You can go free from death to life, and there is much more but Jesus is the name above every name and He will come against all evil and set you free.

Prayer: Father, forgive me for submitting to (name the curse or evil spirit). I renounce it and I ask you to set me free and thank you for doing it now. In Jesus mighty Name. Amen.

This chapter was inspired by Dr. Henry Malone, who published the book, "Shadow Boxing." This book exposes the two ways the devil comes into our lives, the five doors he enters through and the fourteen root spirits he uses (the 2-5-14 strategy). Dr. Malone points out how to recognize evil spirits and the strategy of the enemy and how to walk free from them with Jesus in your life by the power of the Holy Spirit.

The <u>fourteen root spirits</u> are: infirmity, fear, whoredom, perverseness, deaf and dumb, lying, error, divination, bondage, haughtiness, antichrist, heaviness, jealousy, slumber/sleep. Also death acts like a spirit. See their fruit below.

1. Infirmity - allergies, arthritis, asthma, cancer, diabetes, female problems, fungus, heart disease, high blood pressure, sinus, stroke and viruses.

2. Fear - abandonment, anxiety, faithlessness, fright, inadequacy, inferiority, worry, insanity, nightmares, phobias, fear of rejection, shyness, tension/stress, timidity, torment, fear of death, failure, poverty.

3. Whoredom - adultery, beastiality, exhibitionism, fornification, incest, lust, seduction, molestation, rape and pornography.

4. Perverseness - false teachers & doctrine, gender confusion and homosexuality.

5. Deaf and dumb - accidents with drowning or fire, convulsions, epilipsy, grinding teeth, infirmity, seizures and suicidal thoughts.

6. Lying - condemnation, deception, exaggeration, lies, profanity, poor self image, bitch, dummy, stupid, ou will never marry, worthless.

7. Error - anorexia, bulimia, confusion, immaturity, doubt/unbelief, cults, false teachings, irresponsibility, compromise your convictions.

8. Divination - astrology, horoscopes, fortune tellers, rebellion, witchcraft, ouija boards, palm readers, Satanism, seances, channeling.

9. Bondage - addicted to possessions, alcohol, anorexia, bulimia, cigarettes, work, drugs, food, sex, computer, television, video games, soul ties.

10. Haughtiness - arrogant, boastful, critical, controlling, proud, gossip, judgemental, prejudice, vanity, dictatorial, egotistical, mockery, rudeness

11. Antichrist - blasphemes the Holy Spirit & gifts, opposes the Bible, condemnation of the Word, rationalizes the Word, opposes Christ's deity, suppresses ministries/ministers causes church splits.

12. Heaviness - abnormal grief and mourning, defilement, depression, despair, hopelessness, loneliness, shame, unjustified guilt, wounded spirit.

13. Jealousy - anger, rage, murder, cruelty, hatred, insecurity, revenge, betrayal, unnatural competition, divorce/division, suspicion.

14. Slumber/sleep - constant fatigue, draws back from life, passivity, procrastination, success blocked, wish you had never been born.

chapter
21

Make The Trade

**Your Heavy Load
For
Jesus' Light Load**

I Peter 5:6 "Humble yourselves, therefore, under the mighty hand of God, that He may exalt you at the proper time (7) casting all your cares on Him because He cares for you."

Now Jesus said in *Matthew 11:28-30 "Come to Me, all who are weary and heavy-laden, and I will give you rest (29) Take My yoke upon you, and learn from Me, for I am gentle and humble in heart; and you shall find rest for your souls (3) For My yoke is easy, and My load is light."*

As I minister across the country I find people who are worried and anxious about many things. There are many around us everyday with broken hearts, wounded spirits and many who are in fear and worried about their finances, their business, their job security, their children, their marriage, their health, their abilities, their education, their future and their question is - will I make it? Can I get through this? Can God fix this? Will God fix this? Am I going under? What can I do? And the under lying thought is from the spirit of fear saying, "You're not going to make it through this one. This will never change. There is no victory for you."

But that is not what Jesus says. He says I have come to destroy the works of the devil. I have come to save you. I have come to give you peace of mind and rest for your soul. Your soul is your mind, your will and your emotions.

The devil wants us to live in fear, inferiority, doubt, unbelief, anxiety and depression.

Jesus gives us courage, confidence, faith, peace, rest and lifts up our head and gives us joy.

What is the solution? What can we do? I tell people **"MAKE THE TRADE."**

Trade your cares for His rest. I have seen this work for many people and watched them smile again and have the peace of God and rest and confidence restored.

Do this. Close your hand. Inside that fist in the palm of your hand is all your troubles. Now do what God says to do - What does He say? - *"Cast all your cares on Me."* So now open your hand and give them to Him - extend your hand toward Him. While your hand is still open as you give your cares to Him, leave it open to receive. Say, "I am giving this to you Lord - it is too heavy for me. But you said your load is light. You said, *'Take My yoke upon you. My burden is light and you shall find rest for your soul.'* I need Your rest, so I am trading my heavy load for your light load. I put my faith in You now. I release my problems to your care. I know I can trust You." If it helps take a deep breath and say "I receive Your peace and rest and joy once again. I know I can trust You."

I have seen many people do this and get immediate relief from oppression that the devil, and situations, and other people bring. Hope is restored. God wants us to rest in Him, to trust Him.

If you do this and tomorrow or next week or sometime later you look down at your hand with a closed fist and realize you took it back. Say "I'm sorry God, I took it back." And trade Him again. Sometimes it only takes once but if it takes a few times, keep trading, because one of these time you will not take it back. You will leave it with God forever and He will totally restore you.

When we go to God and say, "I can not do this on my own, I need Your help," that shows us to be humble. And when we are humble then God will exalt us. (See 1 Peter 5:6 above).

The Bible is full of stories of people who came to Jesus one way and left better than before. They brought their troubles to Him and left them with Him. Parents brought their children with demons who He cast out. The blind called out to Him and He gave them sight. The crippled came to Jesus and left walking. The woman who was about to lose her two sons to a debtor came to Elijah and God miraculously gave her enough to pay her debts and more to live on. The woman who was looked down on, who was known to all to be a sinner came and washed Jesus feet with her tears. She was restored, her sins forgiven and she was saved. (Luke 7:36-50) Mary Magdalene had seven demons cast out. She was set free and became a well known follower of Jesus Christ. She was accepted and so are you. She was there at the tomb after He arose from the dead. She was the first to go tell the good news - "He is alive."

And of course there were thousands upon thousands in the Bible stories and in today's world who are worried about death, about eternity. What will happen if I die? How do I know I will be in Heaven? How do I know I will have eternal life.

Cast your cares upon Him because He will surely give you rest now and for eternity.

Jesus said in *John 14:1-7 "Let not your heart be troubled; believe in God, believe also in Me. (2) In My Father's house are many dwelling places; if it were not so I would have told you; for I go to prepare a place for you." (vs 6) "Jesus said, 'I am the way, and the truth and the life; no one comes to the Father but through Me. (7) If you had known Me, you would have known the Father also; from now on you know Him and have seen Him.'"* Jesus also said in *John 3:36 "He who believes in the Son (Jesus) has eternal life; but he who does not obey the Son shall not see life, but the wrath of God abides in him."*

TRADE YOUR SIN FOR HIS RIGHTEOUSNESS. - Say "Dear God I am a sinner. Forgive me. Thank you Jesus for dying on the cross, I receive what You did for me. I give you my sins and my life. I now receive You as my Savior and the Lord of my life. I receive eternal life and a home in Heaven. My trust for eternity is completely in You. I am now saved. God is now my Father, Heaven is now my home. In Jesus Name I pray. Amen. (Now get water baptized, read the Bible everyday, pray everyday, meet regularly with other believers, ask Jesus to baptize you in the Holy Spirit for power to live a life pleasing to Him and to tell others about Him. (Read Acts 2:38, Romans 3:10, 3:23, 5:8, 6:23, 10:9-10, John 3:16, Luke 11:13, Mat. 10:32-33, Acts 1:8). Seek God for daily wisdom.

MAKE THE TRADE. - TRADE YOUR SORROWS AND SHAME FOR HIS JOYS; TRADE YOUR SICKNESS AND PAIN FOR HIS HEALING, TRADE YOUR WORRIES FOR HIS FAITH; TRADE YOUR DEFEAT FOR HIS VICTORY; TRADE YOUR PROBLEMS FOR HIS SOLUTIONS. *AND DON'T TAKE THEM BACK - LEAVE THEM WITH HIM.*

ANOTHER TYPE OF TRADE. - You can keep your money, your talents and your time for yourself or you can give and seed it to God - He always repays and He does it in multiplied form. So as you give to this ministry know it is like a trade you give to God - He gives you something even greater. *Luke 6:38 "Give and it shall be given unto you..."* We speak blessing and life to all of our Cowboy Partners who help us to continue as we "Preach Jesus." Listen to God - He will let you know how much to give and which church and or ministry to give to and be a partner with.

Shout Grace To Your Mountain!!!

**God's Grace:
Grace will save you, grace will teach you,
grace will bring victory.**

We must grow in God's grace.

II Peter 3:18 "but grow in the grace and knowledge of our Lord and Savior Jesus Christ. To Him be the glory, both now and to the day of eternity. Amen."

<u>What is grace?</u> It's the unmerited, undeserved favor of God toward us. We don't earn it, we don't work for it, we don't deserve it - we just receive it. God's grace - it's not because we are good - it's because He is good.

We are saved by grace. *Ephesians 2:8-9 "For by grace you have been saved through faith; and that not of yourselves, it is the gift of God; not as a result of works, that no one should boast."* (see verses 1-10)

<u>What grace is not.</u> It is not a license to sin. People say, "We're not under the law, we're under grace." They act like they can do anything, live any sinful lifeyle they feel like living and expect the blessings of God to flow into their lives just because they asked forgiveness. The Bible speaks of worldly sorrow and godly sorrow. II Cor. 7:9-10. Worldly sorrow brings no change - it's just life as usual. Godly sorrow produces repentance which

Hang On To Your Hope!

leads to a change in actions and lifestyle. <u>To ask forgiveness without the intention to change shows there is no sincerity in your heart to change.</u> Why waste your breath asking forgiveness unless you are willing to change?

Hebrews 10:26 *"For if we go on sinning willfully after receiving the knowledge of the truth, there no longer remains a sacrifice for sins (27) but a certain terrifying expectations of judgement, and the fury of a fire which will consume the adversaries."*

Grace will teach you. Most of us think of the grace of God as something we need when we desire forgiveness. A closer look will reveal that grace teaches you how to not sin so we won't need the type of grace for forgiveness. *Titus 2:11-14 "For the grace of God has appeared, bringing salvation to all men, (12) <u>instructing us to deny ungodliness, and worldly desires and to live sensibly, righteously and godly in the present age</u> (13) looking for the blessed hope and the appearing of the glory of our great God and Savior, Jesus Christ."* Verse 14 says we will be "zealous" (go after strongly) for good deeds.

It's not God's goal to make you do what is right. It's His desire for you to <u>want</u> to do what is right.

Grace brings victory. *Zechariah 4:7 "Who are you, O great mountain? Before Zerubbabel you shall become a plain! And he shall bring forth the capstone with shouts of "Grace, grace to it!"* He was building a temple; verse 9 says he shall finish it. You may be experiencing a mountain of debt, sorrow, bad relationships, wayward children or a variety of other things. Begin to shout "grace" to the mountain. Do this in faith, that mountain will disappear.

In *1 Peter 5:8-10* we are told, *"your adversary the devil prowls like a roaring lion, seeking someone to devour"* verse 9 says we are to *"resist him"* and vs. 10 says after we have suffered for a little while things will change. *Verse 10 "And <u>after you have suffered for a little while</u>, the God of all grace, who called you to His eterntal glory in Christ, will Himself <u>perfect, confirm, strengthen, and establish</u> you."*

Yes, the aftermath, the conclusion, the outcome of a bad situation can turn into something great when you serve the God of

82

all grace.

Paul, the apostle, had a thorn in his flesh given by Satan. See II Cor. 12:7-10. It has been erroneously taught that it was his bad eyesight and that God did not answer Paul's prayer for the thorn to depart. The Lord answered Paul saying, *"My grace is sufficient for you, for My power is perfected in weakness."* Verse 10 shows the thorn to be weaknesses, insults, distresses, persecutions and difficulties for Christ's sake - and Paul goes on to say - *"When I am weak then I am strong."* You see, first we are weak and need help; then God's grace moves in to make us strong. First we are weak, then we are strong. There is victory with God's grace.

The result of God's grace when we receive it is - conviction of sin, repentance; change of lifestyle, change of destiny and change of circumstances leading us to victory.

Grace isn't cheap. It cost Jesus His blood, His very life. Don't make light of it, but walk in His grace every day.

Receiving Grace. It's the grace of God that caused Him to send Jesus to take our sins on Himself and to die on the cross so we can have eternal life in Heaven. The Holy Spirit is the Spirit of grace that convicts us of sin and leads us to Jesus. Have you received God's grace? Grace is knocking on your heart's door. If you want to open your heart and invite Jesus in to be Lord and Savior pray this. "Dear God, I am a sinner. I need a Savior. I don't deserve forgiveness but I ask forgiveness of all my sins and by your grace I know you will forgive me. I ask Jesus to come into my life and my heart to be my Savior and Lord of my life. Holy Spirit teach me to grow in grace. Thank you Father that I am now your child and Heaven is my home for eternity." If you prayed that sincerely - Tell someone, get baptized, read your Bible daily, pray everyday, attend church regularly.

23

Why Pray If Prayer Does Not Change Things?

(Why Bother?)

Prayer Does Change Things

Ps. 34:17 "The righteous cry out, and the Lord hears, and delivers them out of all their troubles."
Ps. 56:9 "When I cry out to You, then my enemies will turn back; this I know, because God is for me."
Ps. 57:2 I will cry out to God Most High, to God who performs all things for me (3) He shall send from heaven and save me; He reproaches the one who would swallow me up. Selah.

--- PRAYER DOES CHANGE THINGS ---

God has encouraged people to pray down through the ages. Why? It nurtures our relationship with Him and it does change things.

Jesus told a story, a parable, found in Luke 18:1-8 to encourage us to <u>pray at all times and not lose heart.</u> He tells of a certain unrighteous judge who did not fear God or man. A woman kept coming to him for legal protection and because she kept coming to him he said, "I will give her legal protection lest by continually coming she wear me out." In *vs. 6 "And the Lord said, "Hear what the unrighteous judge said; (7) now shall not God bring about justice for His elect, who cry to Him day and night and will He delay long over them? (8) I tell you He will bring about justice for them speedily. However, when the Son of Man (Jesus) comes, will he find faith on the earth?"*

Will he find faith in you, in your prayers. Remember God is not moved by needs, He is moved by faith. Yes there are times He is moved by needs because of His great compassion for people. But if He is moved constantly by needs there would not be any starving children. God is moved by faith. *Hebrews 11:6 says, "And without faith it is impossible to please Him..."* So when He comes to you with your answer, your supply for what you have been praying for, will you still be believing for it by faith? If the answer is yes, expect to receive.

Remember, prayer is a conversation. It is a dialogue, not a monologue. It is talking and listening, not just talking. When you spend time with God - reading the Bible and praying - He will begin to impress certain things inside of you to your spirit. He will lead and guide and show you what is truth. He will give you good ideas, help you make good decisions and supply your needs.

Prayer must be important. Jesus would often slip away to a place by Himself and often He would pray all night long. (see Luke 5:12)

Jesus encourages us to talk with God. He states in *Mat. 7:7-8 "Ask, and it shall be given to you; seek and you shall find, knock and it shall be opened to you. (8) For everyone who asks receives, and he who seeks finds, and to him who knocks it shall be opened."*

In Exodus, just before God sent Moses out to deliver the Israelites from slavery in Egypt we see in Ex. 2:23 that the people cried out to God in their bondage (they were badly treated slaves). V*s 26 "So God heard their groaning"* and in *Ex. 3:7 God tells Moses, "I have surely seen the oppression of My people who are in Egypt, and have heard their cry because of their taskmaster, for I know their sorrows."*

<u>The Question is</u> - What if they had not cried out to God? They would have remained in slavery. (Somebody would have cried out soon because God said they would be in Egypt for 400

years).

And there was Blind Bartimeus - he cried out to Jesus. "Thou Son of David have mercy." The people told him to be quiet, but he cried out all the more. Jesus stopped and gave him his eyesight. People may sometimes tell you to be quiet about God, about prayer, about Jesus - cry out all the more as Bartimeus did. Be determined to get your blessing.

The Bible says you have not because you ask not. (see James 4:2). Then you still do not have because you ask with the wrong motives. But when your motives are right and your prayer lines up with the Word of God you can expect answers and breakthrough.

In Acts 9:35-37 a lady named Dorcas died. The people immediately sent for Peter instead of the undertaker (now that was faith). In *vs. 40 Peter sent them all out and knelt down and prayed and turning to the body, he said, "Tabitha arise." She sat up and opened her eyes. (41) Peter... "presented her alive."* What if Peter had not prayed and spoke to the body. She would have been buried. They would have called that undertaker and had a funeral. But instead they had a celebration.

Two blind men came out to Jesus *(in Mat. 20:29-34) He said, "What do you want Me to do for you?" They said, "Lord we want our eyes to be opened." "And moved with compassion Jesus touched their eyes; and immediately they regained their sight and followed Him."* Notice, Jesus did not heal them until they told Him what they wanted.

God knows what we need and what we want before we ask - He wants us to humble ourselves and know we cannot make it without Him.

"Ask" Jesus in for eternal life and help in this life. " God wants everyone to be saved from a devil's hell and live eternally with Him. That is why He sent Jesus. But no one receives Him until they ask. *Rev. 3:20 says "Behold I stand at the door and knock; if any one hears My voice and opens the door, I will come in to him, and will dine with him, and he with Me (21) He who overcomes, I will grant to him to sit down with Me on My throne,..."* If you never have asked Jesus to be your Savior you can open the door of your heart now and ask Him to come in. He brings eternal life, so if this is your desire pray this: God I am a sinner, forgive my sins. I need a Savior and right now I open my heart and my life to Jesus. Jesus I ask you to come in, be my Savior and my Lord. I turn away, I repent of my sin and I turn to Your way of living. Thank you for dying on the cross and taking my sin away. Thank you for eternal life. I also ask You, Holy Spirit to help me live a life pleasing to my Father in Heaven. In Jesus name, Amen. (See Romans 3:10, 3:23, 5:8, 6:23, 10:9-10 and John 3:16, 3:36, Acts 2:38) Now that you are a child of God you can ask Him about the things of life, about decisions you need to make, He will be glad to answer you. Get water baptized. Read the Bible daily for answers to life's challenges. Expect answers!

Ask For Power - Luke 11:13 tells us we can ask the Father for the Holy Spirit. When you pray to receive Jesus the Holy Spirit comes to live in you. But you can have another experience with the same Holy Spirit for power to witness, to defeat the devil and be an overcomer. Ask Jesus to baptize you in the Holy Spirit. Matthew 3:11, Acts 1:4-8.

Speak Blessings!

There Is A Time
To Pray
and
A Time To Say -

Learn To Speak Blessings

Life and death are in the power of the tongue...
Proverbs 18:21

*Mark 11:22 "And Jesus answered saying to them, 'Have faith in God.' (23) Truly I say to you, whoever **says** to this mountain, 'Be taken up and cast into the sea, and does not doubt in his heart, but believes that what he **says** is going to happen, it shall be granted him.' (NAS) - or - "he shall have whatsoever he **saith**") (KJV) (24) "therefore I say to you, all things for which you pray and ask, believe that you have received them, and they shall be granted you."*

Verse 23 is telling us to speak our blessings into being. It says speak to your mountain. Your mountain can be obstacles in your life, temptations to sin, bad health, sickness, sin, disease, drain on your finances, even the weather. Jesus is telling us to use the authority He has given us.

Verse 24 on the other hand is telling us to pray and ask God for the answers we need and encourages us to believe Him so we can receive.

Whether you are praying or speaking it all comes from faith in God as we see in vs. 22 above.

Genesis 1:1 "In the beginning God created the heavens and the earth (vs 3) Then God said, 'Let there be light': and there was light" He went on to say things like *let there be grass and fruit trees, let there be a sun and moon and stars, let there be fish and animals. And He said 'Let us make man in our image"* and *in verse 28 God blessed the male and female and gave them dominion over the earth.* (See all of Genesis 1)

God spoke this world into existence.

Jesus said that I do nothing unless I see My Father do it. John 8:38 (Jesus said) "I speak the things which I have seen with My Father..." Jesus did what the Father did.

Now, we are told to "keep our eyes on Jesus." (Heb. 12:2) We are to speak as He spoke and do as He did. He tells us in Mt. 28:18 *"All authority has been given to Me in heaven and on earth (19) Go therefore and make disciples..."* When He said, "Go" he put the authority on us. We are to speak and act with the authority given to us from God.

Jesus also said in John 14:12 *"Truly, Truly, I say to you, he who believes in Me, the works that I do shall he do also; and greater works than these shall he do; because I go to the Father."*

Did you ever notice that Jesus would go off to pray then came out speaking things like "Be healed," "Be made whole", "Arise, walk", "Receive your sight", and to demons, "Be gone." **Why did He speak instead of pray?** He had watched His Father speak with authority and Jesus was given authority. Why do we speak? We see what Jesus did and we do the same with the authority He gave us.

I hurt my back one time as I got off my bareback horse at a rodeo. I could not stand straight. My back was in a curve. An advisor of mine told me to find a believer and tell him to lay hands on me and command my body to line up with the Word of God. A couple of different people did that over the next two days. Five days later my back was straight with no need for a chiropractor or any special attention.

Since then I have prayed over many people with back and neck injuries and God healed them. Sometimes I pray and sometimes I just speak in Jesus' Name. Sometimes I do both.

The Bible says believers shall lay hands on the sick and they shall recover. A bull rider had a very bad knee injury at the PBR (Professional Bull Riders) Finals. I laid hands on him and said,

"I command this body to line up with the word of God; every ligament, every tendon, every muscle, every nerve ending and fiber in this body, line up with the word of God, in Jesus Name." He went on to ride the rest of his bulls pain free and had a profitable Finals.

In March 2002 I laid my hands on a lady at a bareback riding rodeo school in Fredericksburg, Tx. and commanded her body to line up with the Word of God in Jesus Name. Instantly the pain left her body; she had MS (multiple sclerosis) for three years. A few hours later she told me that she had been doing things all day that she could not do before. Her husband said that she had been running up and down the bleachers. Before that day, he had to help her get up and down the bleachers.

Recently at a rodeo, Lance Crump's pick-up horse was crippled. It looked like a bowed tendon. I layed hands on that leg and commanded it to line up with the word of God and called the ligaments and tendon and muscles to line up with the word of God and be healed. The next day his wife, Candi, and me went and prayed over the horse again and again spoke healing. It looked like his days as a rodeo pick-up horse were over. But two days later all the swelling was gone and the horse is ready for use again. Praise God!

Everywhere Jesus went He spoke life. And that is what we should be doing. *John 6:63 "It is the Spirit who gives life; the flesh profits nothing; the works that I (Jesus) have spoken to you are spirit and are life."*

Learn to speak life and speak blessings. To those around you - family, friends, and co-workers and others you meet - speak blessings. Say, "I speak blessings to you." Speak life to your family, speak life to your abilities, speak healing to your body, speak life to your attitude, speak success to your business. Call pain out and healing in. Call confusions out and peace in.

When my dad was in the hospital with a heart problem I told him, "All I know to do is speak life. Everywhere Jesus went He spoke life." Instead of taking the balloon test he told the doctors, "My chest was not designed for a buzz saw (for open heart surgery). Give me an aspirin. I'm going home." And he went home and mowed the yard. He had a few strokes and set backs in the next few months but every time he would say "I'm choosing life," he would begin to rehabilitate. When he talked about his problems he would get weak and slow down; when he chose life he would gain strength.

"Death and life are in the power of the tongue and those who love it will eat it's fruit." Prov. 18:21

What you speak is important even for your eternity. *Romans 10:9-10 "that if you confess with your mouth Jesus as Lord, and believe in your heart that God raised Him from the dead, you shall be saved; (10) for with the heart man believes, resulting in righteousness, and with the mouth he confesses, resulting in salvation.*

It's time to speak life. If you have not settled your eternal destiny do so now. Pray and say. Pray this - Dear God, I am a sinner, I need a Savior. I ask You to forgive me. I ask Jesus to come into my heart. I believe that You died on the cross for me to wash away my sin. I believe You rose again and I will too and heaven is now my home. So I say, "I am saved, I have eternal life, Jesus is my Lord." In Jesus Name Amen. Now read Romans 3:10, 3:23, 5:8, 6:23, 10:9&10, John 3:16, Acts 2:38.

Does your situation look bad? Say, "I rebuke the devil and his assignments on my life and I speak life to myself and those around me." Speak to moutains to go and blessings to come.

The Sex Talk

Sex
and
Love

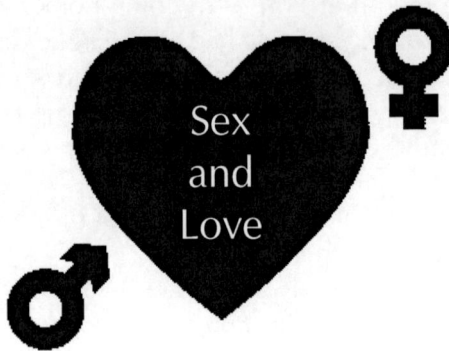

You can have holy sex or you can have unholy sex. You can have sex and sin -or- you can have sex and be righteous.

God designed sex and He is all for it. When you do it His way He says something like "All right, go for it, enjoy" but when you don't do it His way, it's a no, no - it's sin and He cannot bless it.

What is His way? Sex is to be in the bonds of marriage only between a man and a woman. The Bible clearly states that sex outside of marriage is a sin whether it is fornication, adultery or homosexuality. Fornication is sex outside of marriage, adultery is sex with someone other than your spouse or sex with someone else's spouse, homosexuality is sex between two males or two females. You can rationalize it all you want to but the Bible, God's word, calls it sin. No excuse is acceptable.

This article is to warn and help you, not to condemn. The sin is already condemned. But Jesus did not come to condemn you. He came to save you (John 3:17) and get you out of your mess and get you into a right relationship with God, the Father. The Bible clearly states that fornication, adulterers, and homosexuals shall not inherit the kingdom of God. *I Corinthians 6:9-10 "Or do you not know that the unrighteous shall not inherit the kingdom of God? Do not be deceived; neither fornicators, nor idolaters, nor adulterers, nor effeminate, nor homosexuals...shall inherit the kingdom of God."* But you can change. That can be a thing of the past. The blood of Jesus washes all our sin away. *See verse 11. "And such were some of you; but you were washed, but you were sanctified, but you were justified in the name of the Lord Jesus Christ, and in the Spirit of our God."* Read II Corinthians 7 for advice on marriage, particularly *verse 9 "But if they do not have self-control, let them marry; for it is better to marry than to burn."*

If you are in a sexual relationship outside of marriage whether you are living together or not, then do whatever it takes to stop. (1) Either break off the relationship if you know you or the other person is not willing to commit to the other one and have a covenant relationship in marriage, (2) both should ask God for forgiveness and help to overcome further temptation and make a determination not to have sex until married or (3) pray, get the peace of God and make a commitment to each other and marry.

Remember your body is a temple of the Holy Spirit if Jesus is your Savior and Lord. Don't defile the temple. Sin is bad enough but with sex you cause someone else to sin. You do not want to cause others to sin and you certainly do not want to cause the one you say you love to sin. If he or she says that they love you they should not do anything to cause you to sin and mess up your relationship with your Heavenly Father.

Actually the Bible tells us in regards to immorality to run from it. *I Cor. 6:18 "Flee immorality..."* and *II Tim. 2:22 "Now flee from youthful lusts, and pursue righteousness, faith, love, and peace, with those who call on the Lord from a pure heart."* Other Scriptures on this are Romans 1:24-28, 32 (on homosexuality). I Cor. 4:17, I Cor. 6:15-20, II Cor. 6:14-18, Rev. 21:6-8, Rev. 22:14-15, Prov. 5:1-25; 6:23-35; 7:6-27.

Sex in or out of marriage is pleasurable to the flesh. But sex outside of marriage is like all sin; it is a passing pleasure and the results can be devastating. Of Moses this report comes - *"choosing rather to endure ill-treatment with the people of God, than to enjoy the passing pleasure of sin." (see Heb. 11:25-26).* He knew the reward of Christ was greater than the riches of the world in Egypt.

Is there any good news, anything good about sex? Yes, yes, yes. God designed it, He gave us the desire, He gives us emotions and love for another. He designed it so a husband and wife would replenish the earth with children, have a family unit and enjoy each other. He created it for - "special intimacy" between a man and a woman. It's your own special, private intimate thing to do together. It involves love, intimacy, trust, bonding as nothing else will do. In *Genesis 2:24* the Bible says, *"they shall be one flesh."* In *Gen. 1:27* God created male and female and *verse (28)* says, *"And God blessed them, and God said unto them, 'Be fruitful, and multiply, and replenish the earth,'..."* And as for the enjoyment of each other read the book of Song of Solomon. It is filled with the fun and enjoyment of a man and woman in love. Let's look at a small portion here.

Song of Solomon 1:13 (woman) "A bundle of myrrh is my beloved to me, that lies all night between my breasts." Song of Solomon 2:6 (woman) "His left hand is under my head, and his right hand embraces me." (10) My beloved spoke, and said, 'Rise up, my love, my fair one, and come away.'" Song of Soloman 3:4 (woman) "...When I found the one I love. I held him and would not let him go, until I had brought him to the house of my mother, and into the chamber (room) of her who conceived me." Song of Solomon 4:1 (man) "...Behold you are fair my love! Behold, you are fair! You have dove's eyes...Your hair is like a flock of goats (2) Your teeth are like a flock of shorn sheep...up from the washing (3) Your lips are like a strand of scarlet, and your mouth is lovely (4) Your neck is like the tower of David...(5) Your two breasts are like two fawns (7) You are all fair, my love. And there is no spot in you. (9) You have ravished my heart, my sister, my spouse;... (10) How fair is your love." Song of Solomon 6:3 (woman) "I am my beloved's, and my beloved is mine..." Song of Solomon 7:6-8 (man) "How fair and pleasant you are, O love, with your delights! (7) This stature of yours is like a palm tree, and your breasts like its clusters. (8) I said, "I will go up to the palm tree, I will take hold of its branches."

They compliment each other, they check out each others body thoroughly, they chase after each other, they have challenges, they overcome, they lie in bed, they become one.

Actually the Song of Solomon has a double meaning, one for the earthly relationship and the other for a heavenly relationship. It is about Jesus Christ and the church. Who will you arise and come away with? In a earthly sexual relationship it should be a husband and wife. In a heavenly eternal relationship it should be us with Jesus only. Song of Solomon says, "Rise up, my love, my fair one, and come away;" one day we will rise up. Believers, followers and lovers of Jesus have this to look forward to - *I Thes. 4:16-18* *"For the Lord Himself will descend from heaven with a shout, with the voice of the archangel, and with the trumpet of God; and the dead in Christ shall rise first. (17) Then we who are alive and remain shall be caught up together with them in the clouds to meet the Lord in the air, and thus we shall always be with the Lord. (18) Therefore comfort one another with these words."*

The Right Love Relationship - Jesus Christ died for your sins so you would be with Him for eternity. *Romans 5:8 "But God demonstrates His own love toward us, in that while we were yet sinners, Christ died for us."* He prayed to the Father in John 17 that His desire was for us to be with Him. We can. If your desire is to be with Him forever pray this. "I am a sinner. I need a Savior. Thank you for loving me and dying on the cross to take away my sin; I receive you now as my Savior and Lord of my life. I love you Lord; Help me to live in such a way that is pleasing to you. Thank you for eternal life. Thank you for loving me. In Jesus name.

Read the Bible daily, pray daily, get baptized, meet with other believers often.

Remember - Now you can enjoy love, sex and pleasure God's way on this earth and enjoy love everlasting with Our Heavenly Father.

If you are desiring and believing God for a spouse, hang on to your hope. Trust God. He is working on the men to be the husband you as a woman need. Your best friend, the kind that will give himself up for his wife like Christ did for the church, the one that can meet your emotional and physical needs and be the spiritual leader you need. God is working on the woman to be your "help meet" the helper, you as a man needs for your wife. She will be your best friend. She will be able to meet your physical, emotional, spiritual needs as well. Don't be discouraged if you have not met them yet. If you get them to soon, you will try to fix them. God can do a better job. Let him work on you. Trust Him to work on the other one. Pray for yourself and your future spouse to be what God wants you to be.

Never say "I need to be married to be complete." No, you are to be complete in Christ. Your spouse should also be complete in Christ. Then two complete people come together.

So hang on to your hope. God has your best interests at heart. Be patient, God is working on you and your future spouse and at the proper time He will present that person to you.

26 What Is Your Testimony?

Revelation 12:11 *"And they overcame him (the devil) because of the blood of the Lamb (Jesus) and because of the word of their testimony, and they did not love their life even to death."*

See above **"the word of their testimony."** What you believe in your heart and what you say with your mouth is so very important. It will get you victory or defeat. It can even take you right to heaven. *Romans 10:8-10 "But what does it say? 'The word is near you, in your mouth and in your heart' - that is the word of faith which we are preaching, that if you confess with your mouth Jesus as Lord, and believe in your heart that God raised Him from the dead, you shall be saved. For with the heart man believes, resulting in righteousness, - and with the mouth he confesses, resulting in salvation."*

Salvation in a word means deliverance. Salvation more fully means, protection, provision, prosperity and healing-spirit, soul and body. Salvation is deliverance from every kind of evil, especially and most importantly deliverance from the Kingdom of darkness to the Kingdom of light, from hell to heaven. I've heard it said, "You can't have a testimony without a test." Your testimony is your witness, your describing or telling about a thing, a situation, a person or persons and giving details about how God has moved in your behalf.

Everybody needs a testimony of how they came to receive Jesus. Have you got a testimony? When did you ask God to forgive you of your sins and ask Jesus to be your Savior? When did you make Jesus the Lord of your life? When did you experience the power and the presence of the Holy Spirit? Who have you told about these experiences? It is very important to tell someone what Jesus has done for you. It will lead others to receive Him. It will seal your place in Heaven.

Matthew 10:32-33 "Everyone therefore who shall confess

Me (Jesus) before men, I will also confess him before My Father who is in heaven."

Your testimony brings honor to God. He tells us to talk about Him. *Psalm 105:1-2 "O, Give thanks unto the Lord; call upon His name: make known His deeds among the people. Sing unto Him, sing psalms unto Him: talk ye all of His wondrous works."*

In Luke 8:26-39 Jesus casts a demon out of a man and then he was found sitting there in his right mind. He wanted to go with Jesus. But Jesus said in *verse 39, "Return to your house and describe what great things God has done for you. And he went away, proclaiming throughout the whole city what great things Jesus had done for him."* He began giving his testimony to others.

Let's do likewise. I heard Glenn Smith, a cowboy preacher, tell a group of ministers at a Cowboy Ministers Conference that "your best sermon is your testimony." Let people know how good God is and how much He loves them as you tell them how much He means to you.

Remember, your testimony is not just a bunch of talk with no action. It is because a person has walked the walk and not just talked the talk that they have a testimony. First, *"be a doer of the word not merely a hearer..." (James 1:22)*, walk out the things taught in the Bible and God who is faithful will bring you through to victory. Then we can report or give testimony to the love and faithfulness of God.

What about your testimony? If you don't have a testimony that Jesus is your Lord and you are on your way to heaven and living a life pleasing to God, then pray this or a similar prayer.

Dear God, forgive me of my sins. I thank you Jesus for dying on the cross for my sins and I receive You now as my Savior and Lord. Holy Spirit, guide me and help me to be the child of God I should be. My testimony right now is Jesus is my Lord and I am saved. I will tell others about how good God is. In Jesus name I pray. Amen.

Be a bold witness: Now go be a witness, give testimony of what Jesus has done for you. It will take boldness to speak truth and stand up for what is good, right and true and tell others about Jesus. Jesus did not leave us helpless. *Acts 1:8 "but you shall receive power when the Holy Spirit has come upon you, and you shall be My witnesses both in Jerusalem, and in all Judea, and Samaria and even to the remotest part of the earth."* Ask Jesus to baptize you (fill and immerse you) in the Holy Spirit for power to witness to others. (See Matthew 3:11 and Luke 11:13) The baptism in the Holy Ghost (or Holy Spirit) will give you power to come against sin, demons, sickness, disease and every assignment the devil has against you and will give you boldness and power in speech and action.

TRUST GOD AND YOU WILL HAVE A GOOD TESTIMONY - At rodeos, cowboy churches and other events we have seen people get some great testimonies of how God saved them and delivered them out of a mess in their lives. We have seen people, horses, dogs, and cats healed. Cowboys, cowgirls, their families and fans have come one way and left another better way. By the power of Jesus name and the Holy Spirit we have seen necks and back instantly healed, fevers go; also scholeosis, arthrits, spinal bifada, and MS (multiple sclerosis) have been instantly taken away and health restored. We have seen the spirit of fear leave horses and people and replaced with peace and calm. People have been set free from tobacco addiction, alcohol and drugs. Anger has been replaced with patience and a quiet attitude, family and friendships have been restored. These are wonderful testimonies - all caused by Jesus. These things and more are available for you! God wants you to have a good testimony about His love and faithfulness in your life also. He stands ready to move on your behalf. Invite Him into every situation you face. We have seen those walking in unforgiveness, bitterness and hate begin to walk in love toward God, themselves and others. Many brokenhearted have been healed and now have joy and peace and many who were confused now have sound thinking - no confusion - they have the mind of Christ as the Bible says we can have. Believe and trust God - you too will have a good testimony.

chapter
27

Forgetting The Past...
Reaching Forward...

Philipians 3:13 "...but one thing I do: forgetting what lies behind and reaching forward to what lies ahead"

Rodeo's
CLASSIC

Forgetting The Past -
Reaching Forward To What Lies Ahead

Philippians 3:12-14 *"Not that I have already obtained it, or have already become perfect, but I press on in order that I may lay hold of that for which also I was laid hold of by Christ Jesus. (13) Brethren, I do not regard myself as having laid hold of it yet; but one thing I do: forgetting what lies behind and reaching forward to what lies ahead, (14) I press on toward the goal for the prize of the upward call of God in Christ Jesus."*

Don't let your past hold you back from being all that God wants you to be or from having what God wants you to have. Remember - **God is more concerned about where you are going than where you have been.** He not only forgives your past sins and failures, He forgets them. Confess your sin and the blood of Jesus washes them away, never to be counted against you again. (I John 1:9) It's true, you may have to suffer the consequences of it but you will not walk around defeated, beaten down and condemned over it. God will turn your sorrow to joy. So get your eyes back on Jesus and be determined to fulfill your purpose.

Everybody has things in their past that they wish they would not have said or done. Even Christians that love and serve

God and have a heart for the things of God fail at times.

In verse 12 above Paul the apostle who wrote much of the New Testament Bible realized he had not obtained all that Christ wanted him to be and that he was not perfect. But his decision was to press on to what Christ Jesus called him to. Recently, over this past year I have found myself saying this to many people, "I am like Paul the apostle, I haven't obtained it or become perfect; but Jesus laid hold of me for something and he laid hold of you for something - now, let's go do what He has called us to do." I go on to tell them that "in Philipians 3 the Bible tells us that we are to forget what lies behind. Some people finally reach this point. But that is not what it says. It says forget what lies behind **and** reach forward to what lies ahead." And I add this, "Then it says again press on toward the goal for the prize of the upward call of God in Christ Jesus." And I remind them that God is more concerned where you are going than where you have been. It's hard to go forward when you are looking back. Learn from it, don't live in it.

Three times in this short passage of Scripture we are encouraged to press on, reach forward. God has a good future for you and me if we will press toward what God has called us to do and fulfill our purpose. Don't let the devil, people or yourself hold you in defeat because of your past. Determine from this point on you will serve the Lord. In time people will see you as you really are, they will see your heart for God, the world will be a better place because of your life and the kingdom of God will be enlarged.

A former All-Around Champion Cowboy of the World put it this way when he would fail to perform to his best in the rodeo arena. "I stop, I think about it, I learn from it, then I forget about it and go on." And on he went to win several world championships. He was not a Christian but we can learn something from his attitude.

All the men and women in the Bible had a past that needed forgiven. King David, a man after God's own heart, failed miserably. He committed adultery with Bathsheeba, then he lied about it and had her husband killed in battle to cover it up. Psalm 51 is a great prayer of repentance and forgiveness which comes from this incident.   Although David was the King, he and Bathsheeba could have been stoned to death according to the Law of Moses. But God granted them mercy. Their consequences was that their baby from the affair died. But God is a God of restoration and from Bathsheeba's womb David had a son to sit on his throne before he died. That baby became King Solomon who led Israel in peace during his lifetime and who oversaw the building of the Temple of God. God put more wisdom in Solomon than any man and he wrote the Book of Proverbs and Ecclesiastes. Solomon's birth came because David was willing to ask forgiveness, repent, forget his past and press on with God. I encourage you to do the same.

Gideon (in the Book of Judges) had to forget that he was a man of fear, the one who would hide from the Midianites when God said, "The Lord is with you mightily man of valor!" Gideon had to forget his fears, his lack of faith, his past. It was time to be God's man of the hour. With 300 men he defeated 135,000 enemy soldiers. He forgot the past defeats the Midianites had given them - He became victorious in the Lord. So forget your past fears, defeats, sins and press on to be what Christ Jesus died for you to be - a child of the Most High God and King walking in victory.

Peter had to forget that he denied knowing Jesus three times. Jesus restored him. He pressed on to proclaim the gospel and became a leader in proclaiming Jesus Christ as Lord.

JESUS WILL FORGET YOUR PAST - When Jesus hung on the cross and shed His blood to forgive the sins of the world, He could have remembered the night before then they beat Him, spit on Him and mocked Him. He could have remembered and said, "They nailed Me here on this cross." But instead He said, "Father forgive them." If you want His forgiveness and eternal life pray this. "Dear God I am a sinner, I need a Savior. Please forgive my past sins and wash me clean. I receive Jesus as Lord right now and eternal life with you. I commit to follow Jesus and press on to what you want me to be and what you want me to do. In Jesus name I pray. Amen. "Read Romans 3:10; 3:23; 5:8; 6;23; 10:8-10, Acts 2:38. Get water baptized, be filled with the Holy Spirit, read the Bible and pray every day, meet with other believers often.

TRAIL TO HEAVEN

Romans 3:10 - There is none Righteous, not even one.

Romans 3:23 - For all have sinned and fall short of the glory of God.

Romans 5:8 - But God demonstrates His own love toward us, in that while we were yet sinners, Christ died for us.

Romans 6:23 - For the wages of sin is death, but the free gift of God is etrnal life in Christ Jesus our Lord.

Romans 10:8-10 - But what does it say? The word is near you, in your mouth and in your heart - that is, the word of faith which we are preaching, that if you confess with your mouth Jesus as Lord, and believe in your heart that God raised Him from the dead, you shall be saved; for with the heart man believes, resulting in righteousness, and with the mouth he confesses, resulting in salvation.

Romans 10:13 - for, "Whoever will call on the name of the Lord will be saved." You can know you are saved, your sins are forgiven and you have a home in heaven, eternal life with God forever.

John 3:16 - For God so loved the world, that He gave His only begotten Son, that whoever believes in Him should not perish, but have eternal life.

Revelation 3:20 (Jesus said) "Behold, I stand at the door and knock; if anyone hears My voice and opens the door, I will come into him, and will dine with him, and he with Me. Receive Jesus today by praying a prayer like this:

Dear God, I am sorry for my sins. I ask you to forgive me of all my sins; I turn away from them and I turn to you. I accept Jesus as my Savior and my Lord right now. Thank you Jesus for dying on the cross and shedding your blood for me to wash my sins away. I confess right now that Jesus, you are my Lord. Thank you for giving me a home in Heaven. Dear Holy Spirit, I ask you to guide me all the days of my life. Thank you God that I can call you my Father and thank you for giving me eternal life. I praise you! In Jesus name, I pray.

Turn to the book of John and read it through.

(1) Get water baptized (2) Ask Jesus to baptize (fill and immerse) you in the Holy Spirit (3) Pray Daily (4) Read the Bible everyday (5) Confess Jesus as Lord to others (6) Meet regularly with other Christians in church and Bible studies (7) Grow in Christ.

To be placed on our mailing list write us at:
CHRISTIAN COWBOYS & FRIENDS
P.O. Box 187, Blanco, Texas 78606 • (830) 386-4936

Hang On To Your Hope!

To be placed on our mailing list write us at:
Christian Cowboys & Friends
P.O. Box 187, Blanco, Texas 78606 • (830) 386-4936

Additional Teaching material by Ronnie Christian

- **Books**
  - Leadership, Followship, Relationship - $6.00 + $1.00 S&H
  - Hang On To Your Hope - $12.00 + $2.00 S&H
  - Miracles Among The Cowboys! - $12.00 + $2.00 S&H

We also publish
  - Christian Cowboys and Friends Teaching/Newsletter
    ten to twelve times per year

Suggested gift for this publication is $15.00 per year/$25.00 two years.
Add $10.00 per year for Canada and $15.00 per year for other countries. Send "U.S." funds.

To get on mail list send request to Address below.

- **Cowboy Bible** - New American Standard Version with
  Rodeo artwork on the cover (you will get additional
  literature with your order) - $9.00
  Notice: Countries out of USA <u>must</u> send $16.00 "U.S. Funds"
  money order

Consider the above items for yourself or as a gift to a friend, co-workers
or family members. Call, write, or e-mail.

Christian Cowboys and Friends
P.O. Box 187, Blanco, TX 78606
(830) 386-4936
Email: rcrodeo@christiancowboy.org
Website: www.christiancowboy.org

<u>Cowboy Partner</u> - Become a Cowboy Partner in this ministry by sending us out with finances and prayers to reach cowboys/cowgirls and others with the Good News of Jesus Christ. Our victory is in Jesus.

ORDER FORM
Great as a gift!
Order Books for family, friends, co-workers and others as a gift a witnessing tool for Jesus.
*Fill out the form below to order books
by Ronnie Christian*

# of books

_____ **Miracles Among The Cowboys!**
$12.00 + $2.00 S&H $_____

_____ **Hang On To Your Hope**
$12.00 + $2.00 S&H $_____

_____ **Leadership, Followship, Relationship**
$6.00 + $1.00 S&H $_____

TOTAL $_____

Order 10 or more and get 25% discount

**Send Check or Money Order to:
Christian Cowboys and Friends
P.O. Box 187
Blanco, TX 78606
(830) 386-4936**

Name_____

Address_____

State_____ Zip_____

CPSIA information can be obtained at www.ICGtesting.com
Printed in the USA
LVOW100125220113

316512LV00001B/4/P

9 780977 032501